SUPER-CHARGED Freedom

Brett D. Scott

*Turtle*Publishing

Copyright © 2022 Brett D. Scott

Brett D. Scott has asserted his right under the Copyright, Designs and Patents Act 1988 to be identified as the author of this work. The information in this book is based on the author's experiences and opinions. The publisher specifically disclaims responsibility for any adverse consequences, which may result from use of the information contained herein.

All rights reserved. No part of this publication may be reproduced, stored in or introduced into a retrieval system, or transmitted in any form, or by any means (electronic, mechanical, photocopying, recording or otherwise) without the prior written permission of the author. Any person who does any unauthorised act in relation to this publication may be liable to criminal prosecution and civil claims for damages. Enquiries should be made through the publisher.

First published by Turtle Publishing 2022

Cover design: Turtle Publishing
Interior design: Turtle Publishing

ISBN: 978-0-6453953-6-5 (paperback)
ISBN: 978-0-6453953-7-2 (ebook)

turtlepublishing.com.au

TABLE OF CONTENTS

GRATITUDE	v
FOREWORD	xi
INTRODUCTION	xiii

Goals and Paradigms — 1

The journey towards your goal	1
Understanding desire	13
Journal page	29

Your Truth — 33

What is truth?	36
Dishonesty	40
Embracing truth and honesty	43
Journal page	45

The Hero — 49

Superman and discovering it's me	49
We all have a superhero inside us	51
Embracing your superhero	54
Self-image	55
Courage	60
Journal page	62

You Receive More When You Give — 65

Giving and its impact on receiving — 65
The Law of Attraction and its relationship to giving — 68
Embodiment of both these theories — 69
Journal page — 70

Age Is No Barrier — 73

Is it too late? — 73
The key to changing our thinking — 74
Is it possible for you? — 75
You're in good company — 77
Sometimes impact takes time — 78
Life lessons and their use when older — 79
Journal page — 82

Belief — 85

What it means to me — 85
The most important ingredient — 87
How do we create it? — 88
The power of belief — 91
Journal page — 94

Guidance — 97

My decision to get help — 97
Bob Proctor's journey — 99
Finding your own mentor — 101
Masterminding — 102
Journal page — 104

This book is dedicated to my best friend of 32 years 'Kon Giahos', who left this earth on my birthday, the 19th of December, 2021.

He has supported me through many ups and downs in life and not once has he flung me to the side. He was and will continue to be, an angel to me.

SPECIAL BONUS

Download your FREE copy of Brett's TRIPLE BESTSELLING book - I Fly

Get FREE access

SCAN WITH YOUR CAMERA OR GO TO

superchargedfreedom.com

GRATITUDE

This book would not have been created if not for a few people who have been instrumental in my journey thus far, and I'd like to thank a few of them.

Wendy Scott – My mother, the one person who has always backed me, supported me and believed I had the ability to become whoever and whatever I desired to be. Shame we didn't understand "paradigms" back in the early years. But seriously, you are an angel on earth.

Elissa Scott – My ex-wife and mother to my son Orlando, who during our marriage was always a genuine rock and gave it her all, despite the obstacles I threw in her way. The amazing woman she is, Elissa allowed me to repair our broken bond and is an amazing mother to Ollie. She continues to be a great support to me today. Thank you.

Kon Giahos and Dan Verheyen – Both of these guys have been amazing friends to me over the years and especially through the tough times of me pushing the boundaries of mateship. Love you guys.

Jason Urbanowicz & Brad Sheppard (Directors of Trainer HQ) – I spent six-and-a-half years working with these legends. I stuffed up, but they gave me an opportunity to fix the mistake and we continued working together. You guys gave me the best gift!

Bob Proctor (Author of *You Were Born Rich* and many others) – This man was my guiding light, as you'll read.

For many years I loved his quotes and messages. Then finally I understood why I wasn't able to have them work in my life. You are a genuine guiding light for millions, including me.

James Whittaker (Author of the book and Co-Producer of the movie *Think and Grow Rich: The Legacy*) – My performance coach in business, you've helped me with great ideas and steered my ship the right way. I'm grateful for your impact and excited about the future. You're worth your weight in gold.

Cathryn Mora (Director of Change Empire Books) – This lady and her team have been instrumental in ensuring you get to read this book. We simply wouldn't be reading this right now without her. Cathryn personally helped me re-write it. Amazing advice and guidance!

Abundance — 107

A lack of money isn't the problem	107
Your money patterns	111
Get clear on why you want more	111
Millionaire traits	112
"I can't afford it"	114
Other common blocks and pitfalls	117
Creating a new self-image	120
Money management	126
Journal page	129

Self-Care — 133

"I'm so busy"	133
What I do to relax	136
Why is time out important?	137
Some self-care ideas	137
Journal page	139

Freedom — 143

This is what I've learned so far	143
"The cave you fear to enter holds the treasure you seek"	145
Ideas of how to free yourself	147
What's next?	148
Journal page	150

AFTERWORD	153
ABOUT THE AUTHOR	155

FOREWORD

Dear Reader,

Thank you for joining us here! Investing in yourself is the best decision you can make, so well done for making it this far. Big things are coming, I assure you.

While I'm excited for Brett to have his latest bestselling book out into the world, I'm even more excited about how your life will change as a result of what you learn, implement, and reinforce.

Throughout these pages, you'll get a front-row seat to Brett's journey, including some brutally candid and raw accounts that led to heartache, misery, and near-bankruptcy. It's daunting to confront our past misdeeds – especially those that have created the rut we might feel trapped in today – but I know Brett was only too willing to reveal his darkest times because his mission is to inspire you to transcend your own pain, embarrassment, and fear.

Ultimately, he wants you to find meaning, happiness, and prosperity in your life before it's too late.

With each page you turn, my wish is that you're equally honest with your own introspection, as Brett has been. Shame builds on us gradually but being upfront about it is not only the best way to create empathy with others – it's the best way to find (and build) your tribe, too.

I'm grateful to have spoken on stages all over the world, but despite how many people are in attendance, only a minor percentage actually want to change. As my friend John Assaraf (who also starred in 2006 film *The Secret*) says, "Help the people who want the help, not the people who need the help." And the best way to do that is to find out whether the people you want to serve are interested or *committed*.

Brett is committed to your success. What follows this foreword is an easy-to-read blueprint for living life on your own terms, creating financial freedom, and establishing enriching relationships with people who can transform your life.

There's just one thing missing, and that's YOUR commitment.

I'm sure you're excited to dive in, so I won't hold you up any longer. I just want you to remember one thing, and it's my favourite Napoleon Hill quote: "Action is the real measure of intelligence." What you do from now – as a result of reading this book – will determine your success.

If you're tired of the same old routine, it's time to shake things up. And my friend Brett D. Scott is here to help.

Onwards and upwards always,

James Whittaker

[Author of *Think & Grow Rich: The Legacy* & *Andrew Carnegie's Mental Dynamite*]

INTRODUCTION

Richard Branson dropped out of school at 16 to start his first magazine and record store. His mother bailed him out financially, and he was bankrupt more than once. Yet Branson has become one of the most successful British entrepreneurs in history, worth an estimated $5.5 billion. He travels the world, participates in crazy stunts, takes big risks, and inspires millions with his approach to business. How does a nice, self-effacing, "average" guy get to this level of prosperity? What did he do differently to thousands of others trying to advance their business? Is he just lucky, or is there a missing ingredient you just need to grasp?

The great news is that all of these are completely accessible to you, too.

Financial success and fulfilment may not come overnight, but there are many changes you can make to the way you think, feel, and live, that will make a world of difference. You may not be flying a hot air balloon to the Arctic Circle anytime soon, but you could be driving that car, having that relationship, or building that business you've previously only dreamed of.

Right now, though, it feels like you're never quite going to get there – like there's something stopping you, but you don't know how to break through that invisible barrier and launch into the life you truly desire.

Are you making sales and earning a good income, but you seem to have hit a ceiling in your earnings, and can't work out how to break through?

Is your relationship stale and unfulfilling, or even on the brink of collapse, but you can't be honest about your feelings and also can't work out what's going wrong or how to fix it?

Do you set yourself goals, and often achieve them, but nothing is really lighting you up? Do you sometimes miss out on opportunities, but can't work out how to change it?

Does it feel like you can have, do, or be *more*?

You're not alone.

A 2012 HILDA (Household, Income and Labour Dynamics in Australia) survey states the lowest life satisfaction at age 45. An Australian Bureau of Statistics survey reports the 45–54 age bracket as being similarly dissatisfied.

But does it have to be like this?

Heck, no.

There is absolutely light at the end of the misery tunnel. While a goal to move forwards provides motivation and inspiration, that end result we are looking for is not attainment of the goal itself. You've heard that glib expression, "It's not the destination, it's the journey", for good reason. The real goal is the man you become along the way. Once you have addressed the inner demons that have been holding you back, and kept you 'safe', even fearful, the opportunities that open up to you will be boundless. Aiming for one specific, financial or life goal is just a very small starting point in a gargantuan field of promise and opportunity.

This can happen for you, even if you don't know where to start, feel overwhelmed, or don't have the money for coaching or personal development programs.

The secret is in learning how to manifest what you want, how to create more productive personality traits, and how to feel more confident, deserving, and worthy. The process and tools you'll learn in this book will help you create success and confidence in any area of your life, and by using them, you'll no longer feel like you're guessing or fumbling in the dark. Ultimately, my hope is that with the tools I will teach you, you will achieve more out of every area of your life.

By the time you've finished this book, you'll feel empowered to improve your circumstances, motivated to take action, and have a proven blueprint to follow.

Through the stories, lessons, and takeaways in this book, you will be inspired to take practical action in your life.

Success for most of us isn't about winning the lottery or having your fantasy football team come out victorious at the end of the season. The dreams of most dissatisfied men over 40 are related to the goals you probably had in your twenties and thirties, when you watched your mates buy multiple properties and businesses, take more than one holiday a year, and catch all the breaks in life that you seemed to miss.

This is your opportunity to discover the real secret to having it all. Whatever your mind can conceive, I promise you, it can achieve.

This book is overflowing with my learnings and understandings of how absolutely anyone can achieve more in life. If you believe that all your longings are possible, take the action consistently and apply what I'm suggesting, and you will be able to achieve results far beyond where you ever thought possible. How do I know? Because I'll be teaching you some of the Universal Laws that have been taught to me.

In my own life, when it came to my health, wealth, and relationships, I was getting a passing grade in one out of three. I might have been earning well at different times in my career, but the money seemed to slip through my fingers with ever increasing speed.

Wealth: Within a few months of using the Universal Laws in my life, everything has changed. I view money differently and enjoy the energy flow of both giving and receiving. I believe in abundance, never feel short of money, and I'm well on my way to financial freedom. I've achieved this through providing a service that shows people how to create the life they desire, so it's truly the most rewarding way of living and earning.

Health: My only passing grade. A personal trainer in the fitness industry, this was the one area I succeeded in without much effort or resistance.

Relationships: Each time I attempted a "love" relationship, the list of pros and cons I constructed about my mate would prompt me to end the relationship within only a few months. That is, if they didn't beat me to it. When I did commit, I damaged my marriage beyond repair. My personal relationships with family and friends were 'okay', but many of them were strained by my poor habits, such as the inability to stick with basic social arrangements. My relationships have improved substantially, and I enjoy rich friendships with quality people.

People in my sphere of influence, who have been living this way for years longer than I have, have seen incredible success as well.

Example 1: Megan Kamei, an incredible woman from my mastermind group, she's originally from Canada, but currently living the digital nomad lifestyle with her husband Aramei and two beautiful children. During 2019, after a few years of learning and applying everything you will read in this book, Megan finally cracked the $100,000 per month turnover and is now living the dream of helping thousands of others live theirs.

Example 2: Tom Bilyeu, not (yet) in my circle of influence, but I am inspired daily by his content. I see myself in his "before" story. A self-made billion-dollar business owner (Quest Nutrition) and 9-figure multimillionaire, Tom tells a story about when he was unemployed and getting up at midday – he asked his girlfriend's dad for her hand in marriage, and was promptly declined. Tom promised him that he would soon change his mind, as he was determined to change the current situation and prove that he was a worthwhile son-in-law. In 2016, when the father-in-law visited the multi-million-dollar Quest Nutrition factory, and Tom asked him again if he would grant him the honour, the man broke down crying with gratitude that his future son-in-law honoured his promise.

Tom now has a business called "Impact Theory", a media company which helps influencers become game changers by developing three stages of their business: community building, incubation and then building and selling. Impact Theory has over 1.5 million followers and the podcast show has interviewed many of the most successful influencers including Gary Vaynerchuk, Tai Lopez, and Tim Ferriss.

Example 3: Kim Calvert is one of Proctor Gallagher Institute's top consultants; the first person to earn the Diamond pin, which is awarded for the person who manages to activate 300 clients in a 12-month period. It was created in 2019, especially for her and now others are following. But what's so special about Kim is that she was a shy, quiet nurse who, only three years earlier, was earning a maximum of $35,000 per annum. This example should prove to anyone that no matter what your personality and financial position is – if you want something, or to be someone, strongly enough – you will achieve those goals and reap the rewards if you are prepared to learn and apply what I outline in this book.

Example 4: Joel Bushby, this legend has a business called "TNT" or "The Natural Transformer" and his business was one of the first influential social media "online" personal trainer businesses. He is armed with an award-winning physique and a lovable larrikin attitude. Joel has since gone on to include his girlfriend Steph in their thriving business, where they have an amazing community, excellent 100% natural products and science-backed programming.

Joel has always followed Law of Attraction principles and been his own unique shining light, that so many others have loved and adored (including me). He gives more than he receives, and you'll definitely be hard pushed to find someone with a heart as big as this guy.

This book will awaken the sleeping success story inside of you and help you build the life you've dreamed of, but not thought possible; The life that myself and thousands of others are currently living.

A life where you have freedom – SUPERCHARGED FREEDOM!

Let's get started.

Goals and Paradigms

The journey towards your goal

"Hi Brett, this is Lyn."

My admin manager never calls so early in the morning.

"We've just done an audit on our accounts, and we have a problem."

This doesn't sound good.

"Over the last 18 months, you've managed to overcharge us by over $50,000."

Silence.

"What?" I didn't really get it. Overcharge? How the fuck did this happen?

"Yes. We are going to have to get to the bottom of this, you've invoiced us for roughly $50,000 more than you should have since you started with us." Lyn sounded calm but I could feel the tension in her voice.

Fuck.

"You're going to have to pay it back."

I felt my heart stop. Or maybe I just wished for a moment that it would, and I wouldn't have to deal with the inevitable pain of what would come next.

How was I going to pay back such a large sum, when I was already struggling?

I had been working as a sales manager at a company called Trainer HQ, which helps personal trainers grow a business through specialised fitness industry business coaching. My strengths were in people skills and responding to the needs of others, not in computers or admin. It was a thriving, busy business, and I'd excitedly sent invoices to accounts when clients signed up, not keeping track of those who ended up pulling out and not following through on their commitment.

Over time, this added up, and while I had unknowingly over-charged (albeit aware of my poor habit of miscalculation with money in general), I was fortunate to work with a group of incredible individuals, who even though shocked, annoyed and pissed-off this happened, allowed me to work off the debt.

I kept working for them in a sales capacity and was able to pay back the debt fairly quickly, in less than a year in fact.

But the moment I found out that I had this debt was like the metaphorical straw which broke the camel's back.

I had been repeating this pattern my entire adult life. Make a little bit of money, gain confidence, make a bit more money, feel the tingle of success, do something which fucks it up and have to start all over again. I'd overspent, under-prepared, won awards, then hide back in my box.

Time after time, I'd done the same things. I'd never 'quite' reached the pinnacles of success I inherently knew I was capable of.

In 2018, I was opening a new gym while continuing my work at Trainer HQ part-time. I loved my work with Trainer HQ. The guys I worked with are outstanding people, I loved the clients we worked with – personal trainers who were growing businesses, and the challenge of helping them grow a successful business in a saturated market. So, the day-to-day work was great.

But I wasn't happy.

There was something missing, but I couldn't put my finger on it.

I would get up in the morning, do my morning affirmations, go to the gym, have my healthy smoothie and jump in my Subaru to drive the 30 minutes to work. I'd crank up an audiobook in the car and easily strike up conversations that turned strangers into friends.

But something wasn't adding up.

Why aren't I enjoying this as much as I should be? There's nothing actually wrong but I still don't feel like I'm happy or thriving.

It was a frustrating feeling. I didn't want to be trivial or superficial or focus on the material, so it wasn't that necessarily – it was a deep-seated yearning for something more which wasn't being fulfilled.

Over a decade earlier, my mate Hunter had shown me the film The Secret, which is about the Law of Attraction and manifesting the life you desire.

Bob Proctor was one of the experts in The Secret and stood out to me as someone whose message I really liked. For 13 years I had been liking his social media posts and receiving his email newsletter ... and one day I received an email from the Proctor Gallagher Institute, which would ultimately change my life.

SUBJECT: Are you ready for a change?
Have you been stuck?

It was an invitation to his world-famous Paradigm Shift event, live-streamed from Los Angeles.

I sat down with a coffee to watch the event online. As soon as Bob walked on stage, I could feel the energy of those present at the live event.

"If you can see it in your mind, you can hold it in your hand," Bob said.

"A paradigm is a multitude of habits stored in the subconscious mind," he continued. "Once we change the paradigms that are controlling the outcomes in life we don't desire, we can start attracting the life we truly do," he said.

I really can change, I thought.

I reached up to wipe away a tear which had sneakily dripped out of the corner of my eye. *Why on earth are you crying?*

As I watched Bob speak, lightning bolts of revelation kept hitting me.

You can do this.

Your old life doesn't define you.

Anything is possible.

Oh my God, you're going to be successful this time.

I felt around down the side of the lounge for a tissue box as the tears started flowing. It was like my heart, my soul, my energy, my whole being, had been broken down over time, until I didn't even know who I was anymore ... and now I had finally been broken open.

I was ready.

I vowed that I was NEVER going to be the man I had been, living a life of failure, broken dreams, and numb emotions. I was going to change and make a big impact in the world.

I knew I was ready to change, and contacted Bob Proctor's organisation, but everything hadn't come together yet.

I was still waiting for clarity on the best way forward, so that I could implement all their teachings into my life.

I don't want to get all woo-woo on you, but I do believe that the universe is always working in our favour. When we are not getting the message, it just speaks louder.

In my case, this was in the form of a message from an Instagram follower. I had been posting motivational material for a while and sharing some of the wisdom I'd seen from Bob Proctor; and one day, a guy named Marcus messaged me, seemingly out of the blue.

> *Marcus: Hey mate, how long have you been following Bob Proctor?*
>
> *Me: About 12 years, after seeing him in The Secret.*
>
> *Marcus: What's your favourite quote of Bob's?*
>
> *Me: If you can see it in your mind, you can hold it in your hand.*

> *Marcus: Classic. Love that one too.*

The conversation went on for a couple of days. I really enjoyed the conversation, and could see that he was switched on, interested, and asking great questions ... but there was no information on his profile about what he was selling.

> *Me: So, what are you actually selling?*
>
> *Marcus: Oh no, I'm not selling anything. In fact, the reason that I contacted you was that I wasn't sure if you had a coach or mentor you were working with.*
>
> *Me: How does that work? Are you working with one yourself?*
>
> *Marcus: Yeah, actually, I'm working with one of Bob Proctor's Inner Circle Consultants and her name is Mariko. Would you be interested in having a chat with her?*

It felt freaky. I had only just been thinking about how I could go further with the things I had been listening to.

That's how it began.

I signed up to work with Mariko, my first mentor and coach. And she took me through the program, which would ultimately change the trajectory of my life.

The work Mariko would take me through was part of *Thinking Into Results*, the signature program of the Proctor Gallagher Institute.

Settled in front of my computer for Lesson One, I was excited about the new life I was about to create.

Bob explained the different types of goals – the type of goal you've already achieved, the goals you are confident you can achieve, and the big, scary goals which represent your wildest dreams, but have no idea how you'll achieve.

I loved the theory, but my longstanding habits and fears – which had momentarily faded away when I handed over my money – kicked back into gear.

Right, what do I really want?

I want to figure out how to fix my life and then help other men do the same. I want to write a book which reaches millions of men, and I can travel around the world doing it.

Great. That's exactly what I want.

Okay, but how am I going to do that? You're not the type of person who can do that stuff.

But Bob's already explained that you don't have to know the 'how'. You just have to want it enough.

I do want it ... But that doesn't mean I'll get it.

This is a classic example of paradigms in action.

Have you ever had a thought or thoughts like this? When you've considered a positive, life-altering decision and then, as quick as you consider the idea, another stronger reinforced 'knowing' hits you and destroys that beautiful image you were building?

This is because of your paradigm.

Throughout this book, you'll hear me discuss the word paradigm. A paradigm is buried in your subconscious mind; a mental program that has almost total control over your habitual behaviour.

> *"Our subconscious mind runs 24 hours a day, seven days a week." Brian Tracy*

It doesn't have holidays, it doesn't get time off for good behaviour; it simply operates all the time, exactly like a computer. Even when we sleep, our subconscious mind creates our dreams.

When you want to make a change in your life, you may start to entertain an idea such as "I want to set up a business", "Create more time freedom", or "Earn more money than I've ever earned". You think, "Yeah, that's a great idea, I want that". While it's in your conscious mind, it might feel scary, but achievable.

It's only when you make the committed decision to reach your goal, take actions towards them, and get emotionally involved in the outcome, does the paradigm decide to kick in and have its say. You'll counter your ambitious dreams with thoughts like "I'll never make that much money", "I don't know to set up a business", or "Relationships never work out for me".

A paradigm is a multitude of beliefs stored in your mind. You don't need to consciously think about them. They are just there. They're a little like a computer program which is running automatically – and you operate based on the program contents. If you introduce a thought or idea which is totally different from the program you've been running, it simply does not compute. New ideas and taking new actions can be scary, so while the paradigm is trying to keep you safe, you'll feel uncomfortable, you'll have doubt and worry, and most people simply give up on the idea once they encounter this.

Maxwell Maltz, MD, in his book, *Psycho-Cybernetics*, explains that, "It is no exaggeration to say that every human being is hypnotised to some extent either by ideas he has uncritically accepted from others or ideas he has repeated to himself or convinced himself are true. These negative ideas have exactly the same effect on our behaviour, as the negative ideas implanted into the mind of a hypnotised subject by a professional hypnotist."

The paradigms I was running were almost the entire reason I was never able to achieve true success in my twenties and thirties, no matter how hard I tried or said I wanted it.

Whether it was being a Les Clefs d'Or Concierge, a more successful magazine publisher, a real estate business owner, or a fitness business owner – every time I had an opportunity to step up and reach the next level in my career or business, I would self-sabotage or attract an external condition for why it would not manifest properly. Instead of reaching for elite status in my concierge career, I quit and went into a car rental role; instead of getting a mentor to help with the magazine expansion when I hit challenges, I gave it away; instead of leveraging my real estate award to achieve long-term status in the industry, I took on another role with shorter term benefits. You get the idea ...

I was on track to reach higher levels of success with multiple careers and businesses, but my paradigms simply didn't agree with me having more. I threw away opportunities, I gave up too soon, I sabotaged myself time and time again.

Closely associated with your paradigms are your "self-image" and "self-worth". If your paradigms are operating to give you results you don't necessarily want, your self-image will be impacted over time, because you start believing you're not good enough to have what you want.

> *"The self-image is the key to human*
> *personality and human behaviour.*
> *Change the self-image and you change*
> *the personality and the behaviour."*
> *Maxwell Maltz, MD*

Your paradigms, self-image, and self-worth are closely linked. In this book, we'll explore how to address all of them, where the opportunity to be most successful is in addressing only a couple of areas at a time. This means you can't address everything at once. It takes time and persistence. I'll teach you how to address one or two things at a time, until they become second nature and firmly embedded in your subconscious, before you move onto the next area for improvement.

Over time, it's entirely possible to up-level every area of your subconscious mind, and therefore, your life.

Working out what you want

So, what do you want?

For me, it was living on purpose, feeling like my life had meaning, living in the house of my dreams, earning the money I wanted to earn, travelling the world, and sharing what I was learning through a book.

If you could dream up your ideal life, what would it look like?

- Would you have a certain career or your own business?
- Where would you live? What would your house be like?
- What would your relationship be like? Your romantic one as well as the relationship with your family and friends.
- What would your health and fitness level be like? What kind of body would you want? What would your energy levels be like?
- How much money would you earn?
- How often would you go on vacation? And where?

This is just a starting point, but you get the gist. Take a few moments to write down what your life would be like if nothing was off limits.

It doesn't matter if you think the goal is an impossible dream. In fact, the bigger the goal, the more room there is for growth.

Success is not the end result or the outcome, it's the journey. Growth is the ultimate goal.

"I'll be happy when I've made a million dollars ..."

"I'll be happy when I get a six-pack ..."

"I'll be happy when I'm having sex four times a week ..."

Do you say these type of things to yourself?

I know I said these type of things to myself for years. What I didn't realise is that while I was striving for goals, I wasn't enjoying or learning from the journey to get there.

When we rush through to reach our goals, we're missing out on the growth, the lessons, the enjoyment of what we're doing, and the learning along the way. And that is actually part of what makes up success.

Real success is earned in little increments. In small peaks and troughs that add up over time to ultimately get closer to that one defined "goal".

> *"Success is the progressive realisation of a worthy ideal." Earl Nightingale*

Besides, have you ever reached a goal and immediately felt underwhelmed?

My book coach Cat Mora, who is helping me bring this book to life, shared her experience.

"When I published my first book, I knew that most self-published authors sell less than 100 copies ... so I declared that I would be happy if I sold 100 copies. As soon as my pre-sales hit 100, I changed my mind. 'I'll be happy when I sell 500 copies,' I said. When the sales counter reached 500, I immediately decided I'd need to sell 1,000 copies to feel like I'd really made it."

Does this sound familiar? The moment you reach a goal, you straight away move the goalposts? The goal is no longer enough. Perhaps a voice deep inside says, "Well, if you reached it that easily, it can't be worth much." Or, "If I reached that goal so easily, maybe I could do more. Maybe my goal isn't big enough."

You may struggle to enjoy your goals once you reach them, especially if they are within easy reach. Cat might have been better off reaching an initial goal of 1,000 books. Then she could have celebrated each 100-book milestone, rather than feeling a sense of emptiness each time she reached it and it was a massive anti-climax.

This illustrates why we need to set massive goals, and how important it is to enjoy the experiences along the way.

You need to create a big goal and then plan the steps to get there. You won't know exactly how to get there, but you can put small steps in place – keep moving forward (or even sideways sometimes) and stay on the path.

They say that when flying from Los Angeles to New York, it's never done in a straight line. The aeroplane's path appears on a map to fly away from the final destination, but then curve back in an arc. Therefore, if you took off from LA, you need not fear the apparent direction of the aircraft; ultimately, there is a higher plan in place, and you will reach your destination by putting your trust in the hands of skilled pilots. Along the way, you may encounter turbulence, bad airline food, and a stinky fellow passenger whose elbows keep ramming you in the ribs – but if you just have your complimentary snacks and beverages, you'll get there eventually. You may even (metaphorically) kiss the ground when you disembark at arrivals.

Don't be fooled into thinking you must know every detail or every step in your goal-attaining journey. With your desired outcomes clearly in mind, unexpected events will fall into your path, which will test you, help you grow, and eventually propel you towards your goals.

Understanding desire

When you have thought about what you want in your life, the next step is to think about why you want it.

It was March 2014, and for a few years my wife and I had imagined living in Noosa, a beautiful seaside town in Australia. We took most of our vacations there and always hoped we could make this dream a reality. I created a vision board to see ourselves living there, complete with pictures of the beach, a stunning house, fit people running on the beach, and the beautiful car we wanted parked in our driveway.

The vision board was crammed with all the great things I wanted in my life – watches, successful businesses, and overseas trips.

What I didn't know then was how important it was for me to really hone-in on my biggest desire. We would glance at the vision board before we went to sleep, smile at it knowingly when we woke up, and occasionally talk about how much we wanted the things which were on it. We were basically waiting for the vision board, and our enthusiasm for it, to do the work.

The missing link was that we weren't getting laser-focused on one big part of the vision board and affirming and feeling it every single day, and taking small action steps to lead us in the direction of that big goal.

Napoleon Hill says in *Think and Grow Rich*, "Desire is the starting point of all achievement."

There is a difference between a goal and the desire to reach it, and both are important. We want to reach goals because of how we think we will feel when we reach them. We want a nice car because of how we think we'll feel when we drive it. We want to earn a certain amount of money because of how we believe we'll feel when it lands in our bank account, or when we spend it. The "thing" itself is not really the goal – it's the impact that we believe reaching the goal will have on our life – our desire for having that thing.

But this is part of the journey I mentioned before – it's important to learn how to "feel" that way now, and feeling that way will not only bring you closer to your goal, it will help you enjoy the ride.

> *"You must be working towards a definite purpose, backed by a burning desire to have it achieved." Napoleon Hill*

So why do we need desire? What is the importance of it, and how does it affect your outcome in life?

The dictionary describes desire as *a strong feeling of wanting to have something*. The "feeling" is what's required to help you achieve your desired goal.

Desire is the connection to whatever we want to attract in our life. This is why it's important to focus on achieving something we truly desire, which gets us excited, so that we can really get into that feeling ... and this is the foundation of attracting more of those good feelings into our life.

You may have heard of the "Law of Attraction", and maybe you've even disregarded it as some hippy-dippy-shit. There are actually twelve Universal Laws, and while I'd grown up in a spiritual household, I didn't encounter them until much later in life – when I saw *The Secret*.

This opened me up to a whole new world of possibility.

In essence, the Law of Attraction says that in order to get the things you want in life, you must identify how you think having them will make you *feel*, and then feel that way on a daily basis. The law says that feeling this way more often will put you on the same frequency, or vibration, as the things that you want, and you will come closer to them because you will attract more of those good things into your life.

As an example, have you ever had one of those days where you wake up in a bad mood? Not for any particular reason, but you just feel like shit. You kick your toe on the bed as you get up to go to the bathroom, you sigh when you notice that the toilet roll hasn't been refilled, you're frustrated because there's no milk in the fridge for your coffee ... and when you leave for work, there's more traffic than usual and some d@#khead cuts you off and makes you miss the green light. The more you feel angry and focus on your anger, the more crappy things happen, increasing your feelings of anger.

This is the Law of Attraction at work.

Conversely, when your day starts off great, you whistle in the shower, notice the aroma of your coffee, and smile as you glide into light traffic, making all the green lights on your way to the office.

Also, the Law of Attraction.

The more you feel a certain way and focus on that feeling, the more events seem to happen – good and bad –

which create more of that feeling. You will also take action based on how you feel, and the more action you take in that direction, the closer you get to sustaining that feeling all day long.

If you are angry and frustrated, you drive faster, slam your foot on the brake, and yell obscenities at the slow person in front. If you are happy and relaxed, nothing bothers you, and you take the opportunity of a red light to turn up your favourite song on the radio.

This is the power of feelings. And feelings are the basis of desire. It's this desire which propels us forward to live the life we end up living.

If you want a life full of great things – where you achieve your goals and have everything you've dreamed of, then find the desire which is fuelling you, and work towards feeling that way every day.

Having the goal, maybe expressed on a vision board, is great, but the feeling is king. When you decide to start affirming your goal on a daily basis, which I'll explain shortly, you need to make sure you get emotionally connected every time you program it.

First, let's delve more into goals.

Why are goals important?

Napoleon Hill spent over 25 years studying and interviewing more than 500 of the world's most successful individuals of that period to discover and catalogue the aspects which made these people successful, and the one common denominator was they all made quick decisions and they all set goals.

Have you ever jumped in a car and just taken off without a plan, and hoped you'd end up somewhere awesome? Have you ever thrown a wad of cash across the travel agent's desk and said, "Hello, please book me a holiday to anywhere", and hoped the lovely person would choose Fiji or Hawaii and not Afghanistan or Syria?

I think not.

Without a goal you're moving towards, you'll be like the majority of people who either don't have a goal, or if they do, don't have it written down and are not consistently programming and moving towards attaining it.

A 1979 Harvard Business study found that in a graduating MBA class, 84% of the class had no set goals at all, 13% of the class has set written goals but no concrete plans to reach them, and 3% of the class had both written goals and concrete plans.

Ten years later, the 13% of the class who had set goals but not created plans were making twice as much money as the 84% of the class who had no goals at all. And more impressively, the 3% of the class who had both written goals and a plan to achieve them, were making ten times as much as the rest of the 97% of the class.

So, what would consist of a good goal? Start with something you can visualise. If you can picture it in your mind, it has a greater ability to be achieved because we think in pictures. Your goal should be something that drives you, excites you, and will motivate you to build a burning desire for its attainment.

The clincher is ensuring it's big enough. Even if you think you've come up with something really big, it's very likely your conscious mind will automatically put a limit on it, because you've never achieved it before. It will seem unattainable, and so your conscious mind will fight to make it more "realistic" in order to feel comfortable.

This is where many people go wrong. The problem with goals that are too "realistic" is that they don't elicit a burning desire to reach. They can feel a bit "meh".

For example, you might set a goal of earning $80,000 a year. Great. But what if that's how much you earned last year? Or you might want to buy a GT Mustang, and you already own a Mustang. You already know how to achieve these goals. They're safe. They don't fill you with dread ... or excitement.

But perhaps you currently earn $80,000 and you set a goal of earning $150,000. You think, *Well, if I hire an assistant to do this, and I run some ads in that, and I raise my hourly rate by $20, I'll just be able to make it.* Again, it's quite a nice goal, because you'll be earning nearly double, and if you think about the tweaks and changes you can make to what you're already doing, you're pretty sure you'll get there.

What would happen if you currently earn $80,000 in your own business but you want to dream big, really big? Things have been growing and ticking along nicely. You've got some big ideas and have had some great wins ... and you decide you want to bring in $1,000,000 in revenue within a few years. What? Ridiculous. Or is it?

It's a big goal like this that motivates and excites us. The mere idea of getting even close to that figure fills us with spine tingling exhilaration. It also scares the shit out of us, but that is part of the fun.

I'm being glib, but when you think about a big goal like this, fear will definitely come up. All of your self-doubt and limiting beliefs will come into force. You will think of all the reasons you can't achieve it.

We've all been there.

But when you think about it, if someone, anyone, has achieved it, then why can't you?

"If you can see it in your mind, you can hold it in your hand." Bob Proctor

Bob Proctor, and many other successful people who inspire me, talk about the importance of these big, lofty goals. If you think about your goal and it really excites you, but then you immediately get scared and think of all the reasons it's way beyond what you think you can achieve, then you know you're on the right track.

That's the kind of goal worth working towards.

Then you need to use this "fear" to drive you forward. Turn your fear into excitement and drive. If you think of a goal and then immediately think – *Who am I to achieve such a thing?* – that's where the real magic happens.

Rather than standing in our way, this fear can be the catalyst to greatness. Fear can be useful, because it indicates that we're moving towards something worthy. It's a little like the 'fight or flight' mechanism we are naturally born with. You can feel the fear and run towards it anyway, or you can back off and run in the other direction.

Do you remember back to when you were a kid, and thought about what you wanted to be when you grew up? Chances are your goal has gone through a lot of iterations. When I was ten, I wanted to be an astronomer. Not an astrologer or an astronaut – an astronomer. The guy who looks through a big telescope and maps out the sky. They are extremely important people who watch what's happening outside of earth, and can be instrumental in advances in energy, defence, aerospace and medicine.

I had this dream from the age of 10-13 and was super excited to visit the Perth Observatory with my mum. She knew I had a love of stars and arranged for me to meet the resident astronomer.

"What grades do you get in maths?" he asked, peering over the top of his glasses.

"Mostly As and Bs," I said, puffing my chest out.

He nodded. "How about physics?" he said.

"I haven't done it," I said, nervously drawing a circle on the carpet with my shiny brown brogues.

"And what about calculus or algebra?" he asked.

Again, I replied, "No, haven't done those either." *I'm only 13, you know.*

He looked at me with an expressionless face, scratched at his facial hair and said, "If you aren't an A student in all of these, then I'd suggest this career is not for you."

And poof, just like that, my dream was turned to dust. All the nights I'd spent gazing up at the sky, wondering what mysteries were beyond what my eye could see; the expensive telescope my mum bought me for Christmas that I dragged outside to explore stars and planets; the dreams I'd had of working for NASA or the government, impressing them with my knowledge of the sky – all of it came crashing down.

My dream was too large to be real. There was no way I could achieve it – at least not according to the bearded guy wearing cords I'd met at the observatory.

It didn't cross my mind that I could learn all those skills I needed. I could take steps towards my dream by reading and studying and practising. I could take the long journey to reach my goal, fuelled by the excitement of reaching my objective and meanwhile enjoy the learning along the way. I just gave up.

Have you ever thought about something you wanted to achieve, and then either your own sensibilities, or the voice of reason from someone else, convinced you it wasn't possible?

Just know that it IS possible to achieve those big goals. Instead of, like me, giving up on them the moment there is resistance – whether it be from an internal or external force – find the excitement in the challenge and go for it.

Taking action

While I loved *The Secret*, and it was a major turning point in my life, I also recognise there was one major thing missing.

The need to take action to achieve your goals.

The understanding of your paradigms and how they get in the way is essential for you to master. This knowledge allows you to take action and reprogram these paradigms by replacing the non-productive habitual behaviours you have created with more positive and useful ones. Actions which lead you closer to the outcomes you desire.

I've desired many things in life and not quite achieved them. Why? Because my paradigm controlled my behaviour, and the behaviour was to continually retract from taking the required action which would fulfil the destiny of achievement.

In 2007, I won an award for my achievement in real estate. In the industry for less than three years, I was recognised by the Real Estate Institute of Victoria as Residential Salesperson of the Year. I loved real estate, I loved working with clients to sell their homes and achieve top dollar, and I had a passion for creating a great experience for both the seller and the buyer.

The principals of my agency asked me to buy into a partnership with them at one of their other locations. Cruising along happily on a retainer plus commission role, I was honoured to be asked, but scared to death of the big commitment and the move from comfort into uncertainty.

At the same time, a competitor agent had seen my award and offered me a sales manager role at their agency. It was a prestigious, seaside location, where people flocked to buy homes in the summer, and they were offering me a fat paycheque as a base salary, that was about the equivalent of what I'd worked hard to achieve, including commission, in my current position.

I weighed up the options. *Do I stick with these guys and invest money in a new direction which might fail? I don't even know how to run an agency. What if they realise I have no idea what I'm doing? It would be a lot of work, too. It would take years to see any return. It might not work out anyway. Or do I take this new job with the easy money and finally buy that shiny grey BMW I've been eyeing at the dealership on Nepean Highway?*

I took the sales manager position.

A few months later, everything fell apart. The beautiful location I was working in turned out to be completely devoid of buyers in the autumn and winter months, and my wife was driving a four-hour return journey to work every day. I wasn't enjoying the work because of the lack of action, and the whole situation was completely unsustainable.

It was what I'd always done. Looking back now, I can see my years of doing the same. Embracing opportunities and rushing towards shiny new objects, but once I'd established a certain level of comfort with what I was doing, I'd avoid stepping into unknown territory and taking risks.

What might have happened if I had taken the action of investing in the new agency? The guys from my original agency are thriving today, and at the time of writing, have over 200 properties listed at up to $4,000,000 apiece. The agency I went to as sales manager is now closed.

Envision your goal and feel deeply into how you will feel when you reach it. Be excited by the unknown.

And take action, even when it scares you.

But what if you really don't believe you can achieve the lofty goal that just crossed your mind?

Subconscious acceptance

You've probably heard the saying, "I'll believe it when I see it"?

In fact, it's the other way around. You will see it, when you believe it. When you believe strongly that something is possible, you are more likely to work towards it. But believing something new, big, or scary doesn't just happen. "Belief" is only attained once our subconscious mind accepts the idea that we are consciously thinking about.

We have two minds: our conscious and subconscious. The difference is quite significant. The conscious mind is our "thinking" mind; it's where we imagine ideas, it's our creative faculty, and it's where you can entertain any idea whatsoever, and you have the ability to accept or reject as being true or possible, based on your experience.

The subconscious mind is totally deductive, it can only accept an idea that's been accepted as a belief. This means that trying to achieve something which, deep down in your subconscious, you don't believe is possible for you, is futile.

Imagine you've decided you want to earn $100,000+ a year, yet the most you've ever earned is $50,000. You may make a plan of how to achieve the extra $50,000, yet simply making a conscious decision to achieve that will likely not enable you to "make it happen". You see, the subconscious is accustomed to making $50,000, so just like an autopilot correction in an aeroplane, your internal GPS will find a way to fix your variation to the program and return to its original destination of only $50,000. It doesn't know how to operate at the $100,000 level ... unless you practise daily the habit of affirmation of the goal, mixed with feeling those "end goal" emotions.

Let me side-step for a moment to talk about your current personality traits and habitual behaviours. You may be surprised to learn that most of these programs/paradigms we are running were installed prior to the age of about five (depending on whose research you listen to). In our earliest years, we are only operating using our subconscious mind. Our conscious mind starts to build once we get to those formative childhood years of somewhere between three and seven years-old.

Research[1] shows that we are absorbing an incredible amount of information and turning it into beliefs and behaviours, right from infancy, and possibly even before that. Many researchers believe that some traits are handed down through generations, via our gene pool.

So, if they are so ingrained, how do we change them?

According to leading science-based researchers, Dr Bruce Lipton and Dr Joe Dispenza, there are only three known ways to influence your subconscious mind, which will result in changing your behaviours permanently.

---

1   https://drjoedispenza.net/blog/the-waves-of-the-future/

Affirmations

The first, and the only one you have total control over, is affirmations via spaced repetition, which we also call autosuggestion. According to Dr Dispenza, affirmations are "new, positive thoughts repeated again and again in order to build them into the structure of our brain." Spaced repetition in this context is most easily described as repeating these affirmations, writing them down, and feeling them on a daily basis over an extended period. This is also called autosuggestion, because you are suggesting new ideas to your subconscious mind so that they become automatic and programmed.

For example, some popular affirmations are:

- "I am so happy and grateful now that money comes to me in increasing quantities from multiple sources on a continuous basis."
- "I am the architect of my life; I build its foundation and choose its contents."
- "My marriage is becoming stronger, deeper, and more stable each day."
- "I love feeling fit and strong. It is easy for me to eat well and exercise regularly."

Affirmations are said with positive language and as though you already "have" the "thing" in your life, rather than you just aspire to have it. So, you wouldn't say, "I am no longer overweight and unhappy," or "I am looking forward to being fit and strong ..." By wording in the positive/present and *feeling* it to be true, you will attract your desire into your life more easily. This takes us back to how the Law of Attraction works. Feeling how you want to feel and focusing on what you want your life to be like in order to bring about more of those good feelings and situations.

For more information about affirmations or help with creating yours, please visit my website superchargedfreedom.com.

Emotional impact

A second way of changing our behaviours permanently is through an emotional impact, which is often delivered via a negative situation such as a death in the family. No matter the specifics, it's a deeply profound and impactful situation which is out of your control.

Imagine something really devastating has just occurred – in my case, a $50,000 debt out of nowhere. And your immediate reaction is to fall to the floor, curl up in a ball and cry. (If you're not a man who cries, then there may be some other physical release.) At that moment, your brain will kick into survival or fight/flight mode, and automatically try to problem solve. *I'm going to be bankrupt again, was my first thought. I never want to be in this situation again. When I figure out how to fix myself, I'll write a book and teach others how to do the same*, was my next. My brain was already moving me through the devastation and creating a plan for thriving, not just surviving, on the other side.

Another example is from my childhood. As a 12-year-old boy in high school, I recall the moment I started to rebel against my life with dishonesty. My three best friends, with whom I'd been close since primary school, approached me at lunchtime.

"Oi, Brett, I heard you told Lara that Graham had the hots for her," said Julian, squinting at me with disdain.

"Well, he does, doesn't he?" I said, tucking into my cheese and salami sandwich.

"Well, yeah, but she didn't need to know that," Graham said. "Why are you such a goody-two shoes all the time?"

Before I could defend myself and spout the lessons about being truthful I had heard from my mother over the years, Andrew jumped in. "Yeah, we've decided we don't want to be friends with you anymore."

They sauntered off, talking loudly, elbowing each other in the ribs and barely threw a backwards glance in my direction.

Sitting there in my tearful state, I decided being "good" was clearly not a great thing.

From that point on, I tried my hardest to be anything but. I started skateboarding with my new mates from the skate park, listening to Run DMC, and throwing around attitude. Nobody would be able to criticise me for being an angel ever again.

I didn't realise it at the time, but that event, and subsequent behaviours, would impact me for years to come. This is what happens with emotional impact.

Essentially, your survival thought will tend to be positive, and because you're in a deeply emotional state, feeling all the feelings, your subconscious accepts it immediately. This removes the need for creating affirmations and using repetition to embed them into your subconscious – it happens instantly and automatically.

Hypnosis

The final method of creating permanent behaviour change is hypnosis[2]. In 2003, Harvard Professor Emeritus Gerald Zaltman revealed in his study of Neuroscience that at least 95% of our thoughts and decisions originate from the subconscious level of the mind. Which means there's

---

2   https://psych-k.com/wp-content/uploads/2013/10/FanninWilliams.CQ-copy.pdf

only a very small percentage left for the conscious mind to assert its decision-making ability.

Another study by Tor Norrentranders in his book *The User Illusion, Cutting Consciousness Down to Size*, explains that, remarkably, the conscious mind processes at an approximate rate of 40 bits of information per second, while the subconscious mind processes at approximately 40 million bits per second. This stands as proof of why it's important to reprogram the subconscious, and if we can only consciously process at a minimal rate, hypnosis seems a logical step.

Hypnosis is usually administered by a psychologist, psychotherapist or trained hypnotherapist. Simply put, hypnosis is a state of highly focused attention or concentration, often associated with relaxation and heightened suggestibility. Not everyone can be hypnotised, usually those who are trusting, and more intuitive, which is around two-thirds of adults. A person's attention will be so focused, often called a "trance-like" state, that anything going on around the person will be temporarily blocked out or ignored.

Dr. Bruce Lipton PhD, recommends a type of hypnosis called Psych-K which was created by Rob Williams over 27 years ago. This technique has been proven to get to the root cause of certain beliefs in the subconscious mind and change them. (psych-k.com)

Journal page

> *"Setting goals is the first step in turning the invisible into the visible."* Tony Robbins

- How is your goal journey going? What is something big that both excites you and scares you, that you could choose to go after?
- Have you got your goal written down?
- What action steps will you take to get to your goal? Create a plan. Remember, the plan can change as much as required, the goal stays the same!
- What subconscious beliefs are controlling your current results?
- Which non-serving habits are you going to change? What part of your paradigm really needs cleaning up?
- If there truly was no limitation to your abilities, what would you LOVE to do?
- Write out a list of beliefs which then become behaviours i.e. habits you emit that you know are getting you the outcomes/results you do not want. With that list, write the opposite on another sheet of paper, burn the negative (1st list) and then number the positive in order of most important and work on each one for 30 days or until they're a new belief/behaviour and of course, result!

Super-Charged Freedom

Goals and Paradigms

Super-Charged Freedom

Your Truth

It's 3am. I open the front door and close it softly behind me. I creep into the kitchen and open the fridge. The light from the fridge serves as my guide so that I can sneak around and do what I need to, without disturbing Elissa.

If I drink a bottle of water and take some ibuprofen, I won't be hungover tomorrow.

Images from my night are running through my mind. Loud, pulsating music, strobing lights, party pills and plenty of drinks to wash them down with. I had been out with my mate, who was always the life of the party, and we'd strutted our way through a handful of clubs before tumbling into a taxi when we'd finally run out of cash.

"I'm heading over to Doug's place to have a few drinks and play pool. If I drink too much I'll stay over," I'd said to my wife after dinner the night before. "We might go to the pub, but I doubt it."

Doug and I had already planned a big night, just like the ones we usually had, but as usual, I didn't want to tell my wife. I knew she wouldn't approve, so it was easier to avoid an argument by playing down my plans for the night. Of course, I didn't actually give her the opportunity to react differently, because I never gave her the full story.

A few hours later, I'm sitting at the counter, drinking juice and no doubt looking shady as hell.

"Hey, babe, how was your night?" Elissa says as she breezes into the kitchen for her breakfast.

"Oh, pretty uneventful," I say, looking down. "I had a bit too much to drink, so I slept on Doug's couch for a bit."

She comes over to give me a kiss and then disappears to get ready for work.

What she doesn't know won't hurt her, and I haven't cheated or done anything wrong, so it's fine.

I'm just having fun.

***

This pretty much describes every weekend at that stage of my life. I wasn't living my truth. I wasn't honest with my wife about the kind of fun I liked to have, because I knew she wouldn't accept it. I loved her more than words, and I didn't want to put myself in a position where she might leave, because she didn't approve of my behaviour.

Rather than changing the behaviour or being honest with her – to give her the opportunity to talk it through – I just continued doing what I wanted to do, and kept her in the dark.

I wasn't being honest with myself about how I wanted to live, and I wasn't being honest with her. In that situation, nobody wins.

Does this sound familiar? You may not be partying with your mates, but maybe you're watching porn, spending too much money, gambling, or staying in touch with ex-girlfriends.

You can't be honest with your partner, your family, or your colleagues, because you are too afraid of the ramifications.

Why is this a problem? Lots of people live this way, right?

Think about drug addiction. For many people, taking drugs habitually is something which only affects the drug-taker. However, there are other, far-reaching impacts. That person might commit crimes to get the money to buy the drugs, their family may be in disarray, they may come home and be violent with their partner, spend their family's money on drugs instead of bills and necessities, and there is a larger cost to society of catering for drug addicts in hospitals, addiction centres, and far, far more.

So, personal drug addiction, at surface-level, may not appear to directly harm others, but its impact is far-reaching.

I use this as an example, because we often judge our own behaviours, our small decisions, our day-to-day habits, as not impacting our lives, much less other people. We think that they're just little vices that don't affect others, and besides, if we were perfect, everybody would be so intimidated, we'd have no friends. We don't think there's a need to change or get help. We don't want to admit our flaws to our loved ones. We just continue the behaviours and get on with our life.

What we don't realise is that when we're being dishonest with ourselves in this way, we're not in alignment with our core values. We're not in harmony with the universe; and we won't bring more of the good things we desire into our life.

The universe doesn't judge you about whether something is "good" or "bad", but it will judge whether you're being honest with yourself. It does respond to your vibration. Everything has its own frequency and operates at a certain vibration. If you're not operating at your highest frequency and vibration, it will be very difficult for you to attract and keep what you desire in your life.

> *"I fully realise no wealth or position can long endure unless built upon truth and justice." Napoleon Hill, Self-Confidence Formula*

Why are truth and honesty important in your quest for success?

Because truth and honesty are both habitual behaviours. Being truthful is simply delivering what you believe is true. Being honest is not offering anything to anyone that is dishonest. Why? Because you allow yourself internally to expand. When you do the opposite, it's like placing a roadblock on momentum. Think about a time when you let go of being angry at someone and offered forgiveness, you immediately felt like you could move forward, right? It's very similar and has amazing positive responses in life.

What is truth?

Historically, people with power and money tend to have the most followers. Truth, humility, and sacrifice are often not valued.

That was until Gandhi.

Your Truth

In May 1893, a steam train was shuffling towards Pretoria, South Africa. Mahatma Gandhi was on his way there from Mumbai, about to start his career as a lawyer. "Get out of this seat, you filthy Indian," grumbled a white passenger. Gandhi refused and hence was forcibly removed at Maritzburg station.

According to this account, while contemplating what had just taken place over his skin colour, and while brooding and freezing, Mohandas "Mahatma" Gandhi started his pursuit of truth and firmness, or passive resistance. Working as a lawyer and lobbying government, Gandhi led India to economic independence in the 1930s, however Britain wouldn't let go until 1947, where it split the country into Muslims and Hindus; a move Gandhi only agreed to in the hope they would finally resolve their differences and have peace. In 1948, an extremist Hindu shot Gandhi dead and almost one million people showed up the next day, following the procession to Gandhi's cremation on the banks of the Holy Jumna River.

Gandhi's passionate pursuit of peace and truth gained him a massive following, and he was the most famous and well-respected non-powerful and non-wealthy person in the world. I believe people were drawn to Gandhi because of his pure approach to having an influence. Maybe in him, they saw themselves as they would like to be.

Truth certainly has its value.

In my own life, particularly in my pre-rebellious years, there were plenty of opportunities to be truthful. Sitting in class in grade seven English, my teacher was writing on the blackboard. "Sir, that's not true," I said to his spelling of "organisation". "My mum said it's 'organization' with a 'z'." Growing up with a single mum, she was my source of truth. The wise woman who had brought me up to question, grow, and flourish. In reality, I'm unsure whether she told me "z" or whether it was simply something I watched on Sesame Street years earlier, but the fact remains, I believed this was true.

He glared at me, cheeks turning red. "This is in the curriculum, Brett. Don't argue with things you don't understand."

Do you have memories like that? Where you've been taught an idea and a teacher or someone of authority tells you that you're wrong?

In this situation, which is the truth? How do you know?

Is truth the same as "honesty"? Some would argue they're different. I believe they're related, but there is a subtle difference. "Being honest" is not telling lies and "being truthful" is speaking what is true to you, which could include lies you are unknowingly telling yourself.

Imagine you're an actor, and winning an Oscar is your goal. You're a good actor, you've been in a few good shows, and you've got some talent, so it's still a huge goal, but it's plausible at least. Now, add into this picture the fact that your actor friends, agent, and family all tell you that you're a good actor, but it seems a little unrealistic to reach for this goal, as you've never been in any notable film projects and you seem to get cast in the same type of roles.

This is honest feedback, right? Is it the truth? It's true in their minds, but you've heard the stories of people like Jim Carrey who worked as a janitor and a security guard and was a struggling comedian before finally getting a break in the hit show *In Living Color*. Or how *Sex and the City* star, Sarah Jessica Parker, was born and raised in a coal mining town in Ohio, the youngest of four children, until her mother remarried a truck driver and another four children followed. She managed to find success at a young age, but it was definitely against the odds. Comedian Eric Bana appeared to come out of nowhere when he made his transition from Australian comedy TV shows and the funny film, *The Castle*, to be cast as the hero character Bruce Banner, who turns green when he gets mad in *The Hulk*.

Let's break down your current situation, related to your Oscar dreams.

- **Honest account of your situation:** You do not have the experience, exposure, or opportunity to win an Oscar.
- **Lies you are unknowingly telling yourself:** *I'm not good enough to win. I'm not talented enough. I can't get Oscar-worthy roles here in Australia. I'm too old to start a professional acting career.*
- **Truth:** You have a desire to win an Oscar. You have the dedication, commitment, and hunger to improve your acting, get more film experience, perhaps relocate to Hollywood (or get an artist's visa), and you can imagine yourself onstage accepting it.

Although your current situation might be perceived to lead to a certain outcome – e.g. as a relatively unknown actor, you are unlikely to win an Oscar – and the people who give you "honest" feedback are looking at this as truth or reality, what is the truth?

The truth of your ability to succeed is completely up to you.

My truth may not be the same as yours.

But the same principles apply to us both. The more you embody the truth of what you want to *be* or *have* in your life, the faster you will attract those desires into your life. If someone, anyone, can win an Oscar, why can't you? It *is* possible. Once you are not blocking yourself from the full extent of your potential, you've removed the shackles and enabled yourself to move forward. Limiting yourself by some dim perception of "honesty" or "reality" is like having wings which are weighed down with water. Once the wings are dry and you embrace your full potential, you can fly.

Make a decision to discover what your truth is. Are you being truthful with what you really want? Are you telling yourself lies about your potential and possibilities? Are you being derailed by what is currently "honest"?

One of the ways you can uncover your truth is by journaling. I've included journal pages in this book to help.

"Truth" in this context is primarily about your goals and dreams, and the courage to believe that they are real and possible.

Truth in a related context is about being truthful with where you're at, what you're doing, how you feel, and why you do the things you do. In line with this, it's also related to what you say to other people, and if you are truthful with others in the pursuit of living your life and getting what you want.

If you're not being truthful with yourself, or others, are you being dishonest?

Dishonesty

"No Liss, I don't have any outstanding parking fines," I declared, knowing full well that I did. Elissa had seen the discarded Council envelope in the bin and wondered what had been in there. She knew my recklessness with parking, and I'd racked up my fair share of fines over the years.

I reasoned with myself that I'd pay them off without her knowing and I didn't want her worrying. It was a load of BS, but I simply didn't want to get into an argument. I hated listening to a lecture and defending myself, so it was easier to say what I needed to get through. And I was an expert at justifying my behaviour, especially to myself.

Isn't dishonesty the opposite of truth? No. I know what you're thinking; we just went through all of this in the last section, didn't we? Yes and no.

If you truly want to break free of your past and have a successful future, I really want you to start to comprehend what "dishonesty" means for you. Do you find yourself telling "white lies"? Do you hear yourself telling someone something you feel they want to hear, rather than giving them your honest opinion? Do you choose what you say – "lies" – to avoid getting into an argument?

This might not be relevant for you, and dishonesty may not be one of your habits. If, however, you can relate to one or all of these, or can think up more appropriate scenarios, then I want you to start considering each of your own past examples of dishonesty.

Create a list of times when you were deliberately dishonest and then write down the outcomes from doing/saying what you did. Next to it, in a second column, what are the possibilities if you had chosen to be honest instead?

Here are some examples:

Dishonest thing

- Spent joint account money without talking to partner.
- Called in sick when you weren't because you wanted to attend a party.
- Added skills to resumé that weren't true.

Outcome(s)

- Argument to ensue, trust broken, short-term satisfaction.
- Get caught out, someone mentions they saw you at the party.
- Landed the role, tested on fake skill and lose job.

Possible outcome if I was honest

- Partner saying, "Yes, happy you asked," or offering more funds to get something even better than you intended.
- Offered the day off because you were upfront or even given a free day as a thank you for your extra effort given lately.
- Still got the job because they liked how you presented or you didn't land that job, but they had another role that suited your skillset.

When we choose not to tell the truth in every situation, we are generally making an assumption on the potential outcome based on our past experiences and habitual behaviour. The crazy thing is, you might upset people by being honest, but they are more likely to forgive you than how they would react if they found out later that you'd lied. Most people hate being lied to and will hold a grudge longer, or form harsher judgements against you, than if you initially told an unpleasant truth they had to deal with. And this way, you will both know that you did the right thing.

I spent 39 years trying to control outcomes via my dishonesty, with other people for sure, but mostly with myself. Sounds crazy to say out loud, but I actually felt in those moments that it was better for me and the other person to not create drama by being truthful.

Then, in August 2014, with one phone call from my manager about my $50,000 debt, it all came to an abrupt halt. The debt may not have been directly as a result of dishonesty because it was a genuine mistake due to my poor accounting habits, but it helped me to realise that I alone was the reason my life was such a ridiculous roller coaster. It was my own fault that the downward descent of the coaster came off the rails and crashed into a fiery ball.

I'll be forever grateful I caused that crash, as I would not be here telling you the story and helping you "break-free" if I hadn't.

Embracing truth and honesty

When you take hold of your use of truth and honesty, you are actually in full control of your life and destiny. You are in control, not only of what happens in your life, but also how you feel. You will feel happier in general, because you will know your actions are always coming from a place of integrity.

Whenever you are making decisions about your actions, you are always thinking about what the outcome might be. *What will she do/say if I say that? What will he do if I show him the problem?* You can easily spend your life worrying about what ifs and maybes.

On the other hand, when you choose honesty and truthfulness, you can focus instead on how it makes you feel. The choice to be honest and truthful just feels good. And when you feel good, you bring more situations and events into your life, which also makes you feel good.

***

In my quest for enlightenment, I have done a lot of reading. One group of authors captured my interest with their five agreements (Ruiz et al, 2012). The five agreements are:

- Be impeccable with your words.
- Don't take things personally.
- Don't make assumptions.
- Always do your best.
- Be sceptical, but learn to listen.

I love them all – and they are so simple – but the first one has stood out to me in my time of growth. **Be impeccable with your words.** To me, this means having integrity with how you speak to others, making a commitment and sticking to it, and ensuring truth in everything you say and do.

I was working as a concierge at a five-star hotel in Melbourne in the 90s, where a well-known Australian TV commercial celebrity with his own line of products stayed with us on a regular basis.

This one fateful night, a poor unsuspecting room service attendant received a call from the star asking for them to attend his room, as he wanted to show them something. That something was to be a whole cooked chicken being booted down the hall at the attendant in a rage. "Tell the bloody chef to cook this thing properly, for fuck's sake!" he yelled, followed by a tirade of even more colourful language.

As a man, as a celebrity, as a human – he was not impeccable with his words.

Let's do better.

Journal page

> *"Truth will always be truth, regardless of lack of understanding, disbelief, or ignorance." W. Clement Stone*

- How truthful are you with yourself?
- What untruths have you been telling yourself?
- Growing up, we are told all sorts of untruths. What are some that you remember, which you feel don't serve you? Example – money doesn't grow on trees (which teaches us that money is limited.)
- Have you ever told a lie? If so, what are some that you know are not healthy?
- How does being truthful help you with your goal?
- Do the exercise outlined in this chapter. Choose a decision that you could lie about or tell the truth and what the outcome would be in either column.
- I've found that by stating aloud positive attributes I'd like to have, even physical ones, that by stating them consistently and daily, with feeling, I started to see and feel myself differently externally. What are some new parts of you that would help you become stronger within yourself? Example: more caring, more focused, physically look better?

Super-Charged Freedom

Your Truth

The Hero

Superman and discovering it's me

Can you recall your favourite character growing up? Some kids at my school liked GI-Joe, Barbie, Wonder Woman or Batman (like my son) and I personally loved He-Man and Star Wars characters like Luke Skywalker. But Superman was always my number one.

When I was around 10 years-old, living in Perth, Western Australia, I used to have amazing dreams of flying with Superman. In one dream, I was at Disneyland and he flew down and said, "Take my hand," and we soared up into the air. It was truly as if it had happened, and I still remember it like it was yesterday.

The feeling of flying was incredibly liberating. Feeling free and having a birds'-eye view of the world gave me a rush, even in the moments I first woke up and was still partially in my theta state.

My mum sometimes talks about a time when I was 3 to 4 years of age and I begged her for a Superman costume, but because I was so adventurous, she feared I would jump off the roof. She bought me a Batman costume instead. I had seen the cartoon where Batman glides everywhere, so I thought, *close enough* and much to my mum's horror, took myself to the roof of our low-set house and jumped. Luckily, a rose bush broke my fall, and my Batman costume mysteriously disappeared the next day.

On my 21st birthday, I finally got the courage to get a tattoo. I had planned a large Celtic symbol and a North American Indian armband design but decided to first get a smaller one placed somewhere not visible, in case I couldn't handle the pain and abandoned it part-way through. That tattoo was the Superman symbol.

There are a few other Superman stories I could share, like the 500-strong comic collection I used to own, however the essence of all this is the fact it was focused on a character created outside of myself.

Experts in child psychology believe that one of the reasons children love pretending to be superheroes is that it allows them to have a sense of power and freedom that they don't have in their day-to-day life with parents and teachers.

But adults do this too. Many successful business people and entertainers adopt alter-egos and characters outside themselves to step into new and unfamiliar territory in a safe way. For example, church-going Beyoncé Knowles created Sasha Fierce to allow herself to strut on stage with the sexy dance moves and risqué costumes that went against her religious upbringing. It took several years before she was able to "retire" Sasha and be comfortable with being herself in those situations.

During the intense period of personal growth I've had over the past year, it dawned on me that the reason Superman remains an important part of me is that it's a mirror. I recognise the strength, compassion, and freedom Superman represents. It was also no surprise to learn that dream interpreters say that dreaming about flying represents freedom, and that adult men are the most common group to dream about this.

As a child, I don't know if I wanted freedom, but I believe adopting Superman's persona was a "crutch" for me to be more than I believed was possible on my own.

It's also interesting to note that Superman hides his identity and, therefore, the "truth". This is something I spent most of my adult life doing.

Now I have learned to merge my love for Superman with my own traits and see this former obsession as a positive rather than a crutch. I may not have x-ray vision or an ability to fly, but I do have the noticeable qualities he has, such as courage, compassion, kindness, and the pursuit of justice.

In this unexpected way, I have learned how to help other people achieve their superpowers or "discover" their inner superhero. We always have them, they're just lying dormant.

We all have a superhero inside us

Why is finding your superhero important?

Are you in a job you hate or where the boss is always on your back? Being like a superhero will allow you to confidently cope with the day-to-day and push through challenges, or it can also give you the courage to leave.

Perhaps you're in an unsatisfying relationship, but you are too afraid to leave. Being a superhero will give you the strength to make the tough decisions which need to be made to honour your worth – which could be leading change in the relationship or moving away from it altogether. Either way, you'll find the power to have the relationship, and the life, that you deserve.

For several of my clients, the challenges they're facing are related to starting a business. They may have left a day job, or be on the verge of doing so, to open their own business, but they're afraid of failure. They feel that the safest option is to open a franchise or copy another person's exact business model. Becoming a superhero gives them the confidence and power to go out on a limb and do something which lights them up and truly resonates with their greater life purpose.

How do you discover your superhero? Does everyone have one? How long will it take to find it?

First, identify where you want to have more strength, power, and confidence, then make a committed decision that you are ready and willing to do what it takes to become your own superhero.

It's important to note that, for most people, finding an external source can help you unlock your inner hero. This is because we can't see our own blind spots, limitations, and mental programs that stop us from achieving our goals. We let ourselves off the hook too easily. Having an experienced and trained person alongside us to guide us and keep us accountable is often the difference between achieving your goals and staying stuck where you are.

Therefore, the next step is to gather people around you who will support and guide your new quest. Research coaches and mentors online who have either achieved what you want to achieve or have the knowledge you believe will help you. Ask other successful friends, acquaintances, or peers who they have worked with or recommend. Search on social media and follow potential coaches for a while, to see if their posts and videos resonate; and/or go to reputable sources, such as the International Coaching Federation (ICF) to find someone you feel an affinity with. Coaching can be done in-person or just as effectively online using video calls.

I trained with the Proctor Gallagher Institute, who have a heavy focus on how to work with your mind holistically, to change your life. At the in-person meetings, I am surrounded by inspirational and awe-inspiring individuals whose levels of success motivate me daily.

Find the one which feels right for you, and then take action to commit. Even making this first move to commit feels like magic. People and opportunities which were not there previously will feel like they "magically" appear.

The third step is to think about the qualities your superhero has that you want to adopt in your life. Is it courage you seek? Or is it strength, resilience, or persistence? Put on your metaphorical superhero costume and act as though you have those traits already. How would the superhero version of you think, feel and act in challenging situations? Feel into that. Get emotionally connected to those qualities and the idea of feeling that way. Feel the freedom of having those attributes.

When you do this, your whole body and spiritual vibration and frequency will shift, and it will slowly become your new normal. Once you start operating on this new, elevated level, you will be able to meet your internal superhero.

As your own superhero, you will be able to face challenges head-on. You will have the courage to overcome those obstacles which previously felt insurmountable.

You can face that difficult boss, open that new business, change or end that unfulfilling relationship. Whatever you want in your life, you can achieve.

Embracing your superhero

For years, I operated under the same principle – always have a new job lined up before I leave the old one. I was so afraid of not having a safety net, even when my day-to-day had become unbearable or unsustainable.

In my previous role, before starting my current coaching business, I was working with a great bunch of guys, who I also learned a lot from and was grateful to, but I knew I wanted to branch out and do my own thing. Despite the financial stress I'd caused us all, I'd settled into a comfortable existence with their company. I enjoyed the work, and both liked and respected the team. Yet, once I had my heart set on creating my own business and helping others, my days felt longer, and small hiccups that occurred were frustrating and more difficult than they'd been previously.

My future was calling, and I wasn't answering.

Once I embraced my own inner superhero, I had the confidence to do things differently.

I had a couple of clients and the vision of what I could achieve, but I didn't have the income to support myself from the business alone. I thought, *What would Superman do? Would he stay in a job he knew he had reached his limit with? Or would he leap into the unknown and fend for himself?*

I leaped.

And I've never regretted it. Not for even one day.

Self-image

Think about the wicked queen in *Snow White*. She stands in front of the mirror every day, asking for validation about being the fairest beauty in the land. The mirror always replies that she is indeed the most beautiful.

Do you ever stand in front of your mirror at home and say loving things about the person looking back at you?

Now, of course, the queen was the epitome of vanity, but only accepted compliments from an external source. Once Snow White took over her position as the fairest in the land, her faux confidence crumbled. If, on the other hand, the queen had truly believed in her own beauty and other positive attributes, she may never have ordered the huntsman to kill Snow White.

Which of your traits is the huntsman in your life story? When do you let your insecurities get in the way of celebrating another person's success? Have you ever spread lies or perpetuated gossip, aimed at somebody you are jealous of? Or instead of helping someone else to achieve their dream, have you served your own needs and sabotaged them in the process?

This is by far one of the most important lessons any one of us will encounter on this journey towards "Super-Charged Freedom", because there's a direct correlation between the internal image of yourself and your results in life.

We often aren't aware how damaged our own self-image is. It's highly important, even critical, that you understand that once you focus on establishing or restoring positive beliefs about yourself, you will need to go through a process of programming these more positive attributes into your subconscious mind. Just deciding that you are smart, capable, creative, or a good problem-solver, isn't enough to change your life. You need to take action to embed these ideas into your subconscious by reprogramming how you think and feel about yourself on a daily basis.

"I'm so average, and so bland. I have no idea why anyone would want me and I'm sure that my husband is going to cheat on me or leave me," a client of mine said when we first started working together. I looked at the smart, funny, attractive woman in front of me and if I hadn't seen this so many times from other clients, I would have been surprised and in complete disbelief she could hold such ridiculous beliefs about herself.

Judy's relationship with her husband had started out strong, but over the years, they had fallen into a pattern of arguing about her absolute confidence that he would find someone better. She watched his every move, accused him of flirting, and checked his phone as often as possible, just to catch him in the act.

"Deep down, I know he wouldn't cheat, but I can't stop myself from worrying about it," she said. "If I can catch him, then I can just end it and put myself out of this misery."

The truth was that her partner adored her and, to our knowledge, was completely faithful. But Judy's own insecurities wouldn't allow herself to believe that anybody would want her and love her enough to be loyal. "I just don't feel like I'm enough," she said.

Their relationship had reached breaking point. Her husband wasn't able to convince her of his fidelity, and he was getting tired of trying.

Through our work together, Judy finally realised that her negative feelings about herself were the thing getting in the way of having a thriving relationship, and it had nothing to do with the words, thoughts, or actions of her husband.

Judy isn't the only client I've worked with, or person I've spoken to at one of my speaking events, who feels this way. So many amazing souls I've encountered have a poor or damaged self-image, self-worth, or critical self-belief, which gets in the way of their relationship, their business, their career, their health, or their general happiness.

Years ago, I was also my own biggest critic. Whenever something didn't work out, or I'd made a decision that didn't result in the outcome I wanted, I would think, *Why am I so stupid? What is wrong with me?* I regularly backed myself into a corner, feeling down and becoming physically sick from being so run down. I felt an overwhelming compulsion to party, drink, and date a string of women who would make me feel better in the short-term.

In direct contrast to the way I felt about myself, others saw the outside mask I was wearing. "You're always so positive and happy," they would say. And while my personality was predominantly optimistic, and positivity certainly saved me from a complete downwards spiral when I faced major challenges such as divorce and bankruptcy, it was purely a mask that was covering up all the damage that was there internally.

On the outside, I was the guy at the bar buying drinks and partying to trance music, but on the inside, I was doubting myself, questioning my every move, and admonishing myself for any small mistake or perceived failure.

Have you ever caught yourself saying these things?

- I'll be right. I don't need help. I can sort this out.
- If I tell her this, she will react like this, so I better do that.

- I'm equipped to handle this. I don't want to burden them.
- I can't be successful because I'm (insert your belief).

Do you make excuses to cover up really dealing with the root cause?

Many of us don't deal with the root cause of an issue at hand. Sometimes we do this on purpose, and sometimes we are truly unaware that something deeper is at play. We treat the effect or behaviour we are displaying, thinking that's the issue, when in fact, our behaviour is due to a whole set of other underlying beliefs or traits.

Another client of mine wasn't getting the results he wanted in business. He created affirmations about earning millions of dollars, but it wasn't happening in reality. He wasn't even moving closer to that goal. In working together for a short time, we made the connection between his beliefs, stemming from childhood, and his current results. Growing up in a working-class family, he had always been told that significant money was out of reach for "people like them".

Although he was going through the motions for making a change in his economic status, his deep-held beliefs weren't allowing him to get there.

Once we cleared these beliefs by creating affirmations to replace the negative self-talk, he was on a completely new trajectory. Within weeks, things in his life began to change. He landed 5-figure contracts, made more money in less time, and started spending more enjoyable time with his young family.

Why do we focus on the surface-level behaviours or results in our life, rather than addressing the hidden ones? Because they are visible, tangible, and while sometimes those things need to be changed, that won't correct the "cause" of our real problem. It's like placing a band-aid over a broken bone!

How can we fix this? How can we repair our self-image? First, create a list of behaviours you consider negative or undesirable on one sheet of paper and on another sheet write out all the "polar opposite" or more positive desired ones you would prefer.

Then it's time to start programming these positive behaviours into your subconscious mind, after we burn or shred the negative.

- From the positive list you created, pick the top one or two you'd like to focus on first.
- Write out an affirmation for each one, focusing on what you'd like to achieve. For example, "I am honest with everyone." And "I exercise every day."

  Keep it in present tense: i.e. .Don't write, "I will be honest with everyone," or "I will exercise every day."

  Make it positive language: i.e. Don't write, "I'm not dishonest anymore," or "I'm no longer lazy and inactive."

- Write them out every day, morning and night, 100 times each. Most people find it easiest to do this first thing in the morning, before they look at emails or social media, and last thing at night, before they sleep, when their brains are most primed to accept subconscious messages.
- Read them out loud as you write them. *Feel* into the statements, don't just write and say them without feeling. The feeling is important.
- Literally shred and/or burn the negative list. It's a symbolic way of removing these from your subconscious mind.

The process of writing these out will trick your brain into believing and accepting them as truth. This will help with creating new neural pathways and new behaviours to go with these new beliefs.

Like any new habit, it will take 21–28 days to really lock-in and have your mind accept the new program/paradigm.

Courage

The yellow brick road was by far one of the biggest tests any of the characters along with Dorothy would ever face. The Tin Man finally found his heart, the Scarecrow received a brain, and the Lion got his courage. The interesting symbology I read from this is that each character, including Dorothy, all had to go through their own trials to get what they truly wanted. They practised embodying their deepest desires, and therefore did the work of uncovering them, even though it was without realising it. When they met the Wizard to ask for what they wanted, it turned out they had achieved their desired traits on their own. The path they took had actually allowed them to discover their gifts for themselves.

We have all done this in our own lives. Waiting for someone else to give us validation or permission to achieve our goals. Giving the power to others to make us feel a certain way. Allowing someone else's opinion to decide if we're worthy to achieve something.

The reality is that if we know what we want, and go after it with courage, we can achieve it.

Courage seems to build with your self-image, too. The stronger you feel inside as a person, the braver you become when you know you've got to step outside of yourself to truly make magic happen.

Having a purpose also gives you the necessary courage to do certain things you would normally consider a roadblock or a difficulty you'd rather not face. Why? Because your purpose is bigger than you; it's usually driven by a passion or a skill you have, and you have an easier time putting your ego aside in its pursuit.

In the Wizard of Oz, the Cowardly Lion is afraid of everything. To the point he can't even sleep. He agrees to go on the journey with Dorothy to meet the Wizard of Oz to see if he could be helped with some courage.

The Wizard does help the Lion; he gives him a dish of unknown liquid to help him remove the fear. The Lion argues that the liquid courage is only temporary, however the Lion's ability to face fear in times of danger certainly doesn't match his sentiment.

I personally feel like many of us, when we are lacking something, it's never receiving something outside that fixes us, it's what we do inside and the repetition of the practice of doing that which we fear or feel we lack that builds our confidence.

Are you ready to be brave?

Journal page

> *"A hero is someone who has given his or her life to something bigger than oneself."* Joseph Campbell

- Which superhero do you relate to? Or if you're not into superheros, what characteristics would you choose as superpowers?
- Additionally, what's one superpower you would love to have and how would you use it for good?
- Can you see some holes in your internal self-image? If so, what are they? Example: I lack belief in everything I do. I feel unworthy of success. I am not as confident as I would like to be.
- What are some of the positive aspects of your self-image you already know you have? Examples: kindness, positive energy, growth mindset.
- Do you have the courage to change your life? How will you start? List three things to help you focus on getting started.
- What impact do you think focusing on a superhero or superpowers will do to help your inner 'self-image'?
- To obtain new aspects of your internal self-image, we need to go through a repetition process of affirmations. What is the number 1 new belief/behaviour you're going to implement?

The Hero

Super-Charged Freedom

You Receive More When You Give

Giving and its impact on receiving

At the age of 12, I could have written the following about Christmas:

Christmas Eve is here, and I've been told to go to bed at 8pm. I know that Santa's not real, but I still love Christmas Day. I spent the past week finding small gifts for my mum and my grandmother. I love waking up early and racing out to see what Santa (Mum) has packed into my Santa bag, but I also love seeing their faces when they finally open up the gifts I chose.

As an adult, my anticipation of Christmas is quite different. It's no longer the same excitement for me personally, even though I still get gifts from my mum, but there's still an incredible sense of joy watching the anticipation of my son, who wants to get up early and unwrap what Santa brought.

The Bible quote and often quoted saying, "It's better to give than to receive," is not just a cliché. Giving and receiving are different aspects of the flow of energy in the universe, and you will receive more when you give. Most of my life I've been a giver, always happy to help and make people feel welcome. I even made a career of it as a concierge in hotels for nearly a decade. I also worked as a waiter, a bartender, a landscaper, a personal trainer, and a coach. All were service-oriented roles, and I got enjoyment out of giving. I wanted to be liked, and I knew that people would be grateful and responsive to my gifts of service.

I can remember picking flowers for my mum as a young boy, because I knew it made her happy. Or offering to help older people cross the road or carry their shopping. If a friend was moving house, I'd offer to help them move ...

But we don't give in a vacuum. When we give, we also receive. Sometimes, we have a bias towards what we will receive when we give, and sometimes, the receiving is a bonus by-product. When I helped people move house, for example, I did anticipate they would offer pizza and beers at the end of the day. But when I gave flowers to my mum, it was genuinely because I wanted to see her happy and bring a little bit of joy into her day.

Therefore, you could view your giving as a positive, a negative, or neutral, based upon your motivation to give.

While I explained that giving and receiving are on the same energy wavelength, an important distinction is that there is an order to it. The order is first to give, and then to receive.

Many of us are pushing to receive. "Give it to me now," or "I gave you that, so you have to give me something in return."

When you are fuelled by receiving, it's no longer giving, it's trading.

The greater impact you can make on your fellow man in a positive way, the greater impact you'll have in your own life, and it won't always – in fact most times – WILL NOT come from the place you gave it.

Stop focusing on the short-term impact of your giving – i.e. thinking about what you'll immediately receive back. Trust that the universe will flow gifts back to you, in time, and for your greater good.

Do you give with the spirit of true and honest service, without expecting anything in return? Do you give to genuinely help, including helping others without them even knowing it was you? Would you give even if the recipient didn't find out who gave?

W. Clement Stone, who worked with Napoleon Hill in the 1950s, said that one of his keys to success was doing something every day for another person, usually without them knowing who had done them the favour. "Your most precious valued possessions and your greatest powers are invisible and intangible. No-one can take them. You, and you alone, can give them. You will receive abundance for your giving," he said.

Today, "how" I like to give has changed. It has to be honest. I have a no BS approach to helping people as a coach and mentor. It's not about being liked or how the giving is received. It's not about winning brownie points or influencing how others see me. My giving is about how I can truly help and serve. I give in true service, even if it's confronting and they get pissed-off at me. At least they'll know where they stand and that I'm always saying it with the right intentions.

Isn't that the best service one can give?

Giving with a higher purpose in mind will raise your frequency to a higher vibration, and that's when you attract more goodness into your life.

How can you think selflessly on a daily basis? How can you go out of your way to help someone or leave a person feeling better as a result of being near or with you?

True freedom is found in giving without hoping or waiting for something to come back to you. Ironically, you are more in control of receiving and having happiness in your life when you're not actually trying to control outcomes from your giving.

The Law of Attraction and its relationship to giving

- The LOA is about focusing on the feelings you want to feel when you achieve your goal.
- One aspect of this is giving with joy, focused purely on feeling great about giving. Ultimately, you will attract and receive more great things into your life which brings about feelings of joy.
- Most people want happiness. It's not about focusing on "things", but about how you believe you'll feel when you have these things in your life.
- The LOA can also be used to bring other emotions and feelings into your existence.

Embodiment of both these theories

- Rhonda Byrne created The Secret without years of experience and was not fully knowledgeable about the Law of Attraction.
- She was focusing on giving and sharing the knowledge she had, and on learning as she went. This was evidenced by multiple things being left out of the movie, such as the need to take action towards your desires.
- She has received more than a hundred-fold what she put in. She was broke when she made the film, and is worth $100 million today.
- At the same time, she has inspired many others to live a life at a higher vibration, in service to others. She inspired me to change my life and also introduced me to other people I admire.
- I am writing this book without having reached my full potential. I'm in service to those reading and bringing you on the journey of abundance with me. I don't know everything yet.

Journal page

> *We make a living by what we get, but we make a life by what we give."* Sir Winston Churchill

- What does it look like for you when you "give"? What happens?

- Giving and receiving are one and the same, you cannot have one without the other. However, do you expect to receive something in return from someone when you give? If yes, what and why? And if no, what makes you think that?

- You may have heard the expression, "It's better to give than receive." Do you agree with this and why?

- It has been said that the path to your desired level of wealth and abundance is factored in by your level of giving. What does this mean to you? How can you apply it?

- What is something you could do today for the next 30 days that allows you to give consistently, without expecting anything in return?

- The Law of Attraction is dictated by the Law of Vibration. And if everything you truly desire (positive) is on a higher vibration than you're currently on, what things could you decide to do daily to get into the right vibration to attract? Examples: Gratitude practice, journaling, meditation, yoga, exercise ...

- What are some aspects in your life that you'd truly love to attract and why?

You Receive More When You Give

Super-Charged Freedom

Age Is No Barrier

Is it too late?

In working with clients and speaking at events, I've had the privilege of holding space for many different men and women, particularly those facing and overcoming challenges past the age of 40.

I've heard multiple stories of adversity, regretted decision-making, struggle, frustration, and sometimes hope about what the future might bring. Often, however, the stories of hope are tinged with defeatist paradigms about the person's ability to make the changes, do the work, or achieve their goals.

"I've tried so many things to change my life and nothing seems to work ..."

"As soon as I start to see some growth, I fall back into my old ways ..."

"I'm too old to start again ..."

"If I was younger, I would ..."

Do any of these sound familiar?

If so, you're not alone. It's easy to feel this way when you have essentially been living day-to-day, just facing the road ahead in the same way you always did. Going through the motions, doing what needs to be done, putting out the fires, putting one foot in front of the other. It is a rare human who stops to evaluate where they actually are and makes a decision to really shake things up.

Why is it then, that even when somebody makes a decision to change, that results can seem rare and hard to come by? One of the reasons is that until you go out of your way to reprogram your paradigms (and I talked about affirmations as a way of reprogramming your beliefs in an earlier chapter), you will keep operating under your old paradigms. This means that you will keep acting based on the same beliefs, thoughts, and actions as you did before. When you do this, you will keep getting the same results as before.

"We cannot solve our problems with the same thinking we used when we created them," Albert Einstein is quoted as saying. Another favourite is, "Insanity is doing the same thing, over and over again, expecting a different result!"

But when we are inside our own unique situation, it can be impossible to see that we are, in fact, doing the same thing as before.

The key to changing our thinking

If you really want to make changes and unlock the power and freedom in your life, don't do it alone. A significant barrier to achieving change is not getting help. If we want to stereotype what it's like to be a man, it would be fair to say that many men feel like they don't need help. Even if they recognise that help would be beneficial, they may struggle to ask for it.

In my coaching practice, and in conversations with coaches and mentors in my peer community and mastermind groups, I have heard this referenced numerous times. Clients who struggled for years until they worked with a coach or mentor, and then finally exploded on the trajectory they had previously only been dreaming about.

When you work with somebody who is trained in recognising and disrupting unhelpful ways of thinking and behaving, you can accomplish much more than you ever thought possible before, or indeed attained on your own.

Is it possible for you?

Let's look at some stories of inspirational people who have achieved great success well into the double digits.

In 2003, at the age of 70, Yūichirō Miura reached the freezing cold summit of Mt Everest. It was an incredible feat for anybody, let alone a little grey-haired man from Tokyo. Miura returned to his home successful and an inspiration to people of all ages, holding the Guinness World Record for being the oldest person to conquer Everest.

Over the ensuing five years, three more men in their seventies did the same. Not to be outdone, Miura returned to Everest twice more, and successfully scaled the summit, taking back his record on two separate occasions. Not only did he prove that age is no barrier to reaching dizzying heights, he underwent two heart surgeries for cardiac arrhythmia in the interim.

In the celebrity world, despite Hollywood's tendency to worship youth, stories of success over 40 are plentiful.

While on our honeymoon, my wife and I were doing some shopping and popped into a cinema to see a comedy called *The 40-Year-Old Virgin*, starring Steve Carell. Beyond the movie magic of the chest waxing scene and many other embarrassing moments I hoped never to experience, the best part was discovering that this actor had only gotten his first big break at the age of 43. A big year for Carell, he was in the TV show *The Office* at the same time, becoming one of comedy's leading men.

More well-known names who earned their big breaks later in life are:

- **Samuel L. Jackson:** What many don't know is he struggled with drug addiction for two years before getting a break at age 43, in Spike Lee's 1991 movie, *Jungle Fever*. Then, he went on to perform his stand-out role in the 1994 film, *Pulp Fiction*, alongside John Travolta, who was 46 years-old.

- **Martha Stewart:** Martha was well into her 40s before she landed the role of "America's housewife". Prior to that, she worked in catering and fashion modelling.

- **Henry Ford:** Not many people know that Mr Ford was an engineer working for Thomas A. Edison before he founded the Ford Motor company when he was 40. Five years later, he produced the famous "Model T" Ford car.

- **Reid Hoffman:** As we know, many social media businesses were founded by young tech geniuses. Not Mr Hoffman, he was 35 when he founded LinkedIn in 2002. Eight years later, he took it public and became a billionaire.

- **Julia Child:** Ms Child hadn't even eaten French food until the age of 36, then because she was absolutely stunned by this cuisine while living in France after World War II, she studied it until she had enough knowledge to host the TV show, *The French Chef*, at 51 years of age.

- **Alan Rickman:** This actor got his big break as Hans Gruber in *Die Hard* alongside Bruce Willis when he was 41 years of age. He gave up his graphic design career in his mid-20s to get into acting, spent years working in theatre, and it took more than 15 years to reach international film stardom.
- **Ray Kroc and "Colonel" Harland Sanders:** Ray was 52 when he met the McDonalds brothers, and the Colonel didn't become a chef till the age of 40 and used his social security cheques to begin franchising KFC at 65. He didn't become an icon until he sold the company at 75.

You're getting inspired, aren't you?

You're in good company

Napoleon Hill interviewed 500 successful people for his book *Think and Grow Rich* in the 1930s.

One story told of an accountant who applied to get into university and study law after the age of 40. Friends and family warned him that he had a wife, kids, and bills to pay, but he knew that he'd be much happier, and ultimately successful, by pursuing his passion. He completed his four-year degree in only three years and his new career was a roaring success.

"Most of the truly successful people I've interviewed didn't have their big wins till after the age of 40," Hill is quoted as saying. He states from an analysis of over 25,000 people that most who succeed in an outstanding way, are generally over the age of 40, and sometimes well beyond 50.

At the same time as I watched Bob Proctor's *Paradigm Shift* event, I was working as a manager at a gym in Maroochydore, Queensland, Australia. Driving an hour each way gave me the perfect opportunity to put my newfound inspiration and beliefs into practice.

Inspired by Bob Proctor, I had started reading *Think and Grow Rich* daily, like others may read the Bible. I then discovered it as a recording on Audible, and utilised my driving time to listen to that, as well as other motivational books and podcasts. At the time of writing, I have listened to and read the book almost 20 times. Whenever I hear the soothing tones of Earl Nightingale narrating Napoleon's words, I feel a fresh sense of empowerment.

My dreams are truly within reach, and so are yours.

Sometimes impact takes time

There are times, though, where what you have "decided" does not impact on your beliefs, thoughts, or actions, until much later. It's a process.

When I saw the movie *The Secret*, I finally woke up to the unsatisfactory way I'd been living my life and how it could be different. I finally understood my plethora of possibilities and felt confident there was a way I could attract the things I wanted in my life. But I didn't change things overnight. I started attracting good things into my life, but what the movie didn't teach was the entire "order" required by following the Universal Laws, and that by applying these, we have a greater ability to restore or reprogram our internal self-image. This is not a quick fix, and it takes work, but by moving with the Law, you will find it easier to adopt, apply, and discover your power.

It took me 13 years to truly understand why I wasn't achieving what I really wanted, and in fact, I was going backwards. I was in a repetitive cycle of two steps forward, three steps back. Can you relate?

Looking back, this extended journey to success was a positive. It meant that I could fully understand the frustrations and barriers to effectively changing paradigms and achieving new goals. In my coaching and mentoring business, I use this knowledge and experience daily with my clients.

I will ask you the same question I ask them:

Do you feel or have you felt like you are on a hamster wheel? Does it seem as though you adopt a new practice or work towards forming a new habit, but the actions don't last more than a few days?

You are not alone.

Be assured that once you make a decision to change your life, you have taken a major and crucial first step towards reaching your goals. Beyond that, daily action must be taken to reprogram your old paradigms, but help is available. This book, along with other books I reference, and the support and guidance of a coach or mentor, may make all the difference between you either celebrating your successes or beating yourself up that you failed once again.

Life lessons and their use when older

In 1935, at the ripe young age of 45, Harland David Sanders was awarded the title of Kentucky Colonel by the Kentucky Governor for his service to the community – which was not a war service award. By 1939, the USA guide "Adventures in Good Eating" put Colonel Sanders gas (Shell) station eatery on the map, and by 1952, the first KFC opened in South Salt Lake in Utah. In 1955, at 65 years-old, he sold his first restaurant outside of Kentucky and with only a $105 social security cheque to support him, he started to set up franchising across the country. By 1964, at age 73, Colonel Sanders sold the franchise business for $2 million. He kept the rights for Canada and also became the face and brand ambassador – and to this day, his image is still being used.

One thing I've noticed since being 40+, and starting to reach new levels of success, is that I'm less encumbered. What I mean by this is that I'm not driven by nightlife or distractions, which can easily derail us. In my 20s and 30s, my head was turned by every shiny, fun-looking object, good looking woman, or opportunity to party. Even though I was presented with information and teachings that I knew at surface-level, I wasn't able to properly understand or use them because of my over-arching and non-productive paradigms, poor habitual behaviour, and self-sabotaging cycles.

In my real estate years, I was surrounded by savvy investors and clever business people who were setting up their financial futures in an impressive way. When I won my real estate award, my immediate thought was along the lines of, "Now I can command a higher salary." More money meant more fun, more "things", more of the lifestyle I enjoyed. At the same time, the exceptional men who were principals of the agency I worked for offered me an opportunity to buy into and expand the business. In line with my values at the time, I thought, "But that would mean spending my money to invest and taking home a lesser salary." It felt like a move that would take me further away from my goals at the time.

I knew that I wanted a home, investment properties, and a stable financial future, but the pull towards the party lifestyle and short-term gains was stronger. I did have the awareness that I needed to move away from some local friends who supported my less-healthy habits, and that played a part in not sticking around to join the ownership team; but for the most part, it was not an attractive offer, because I was in the fast lane, and taking responsibility for growing a business would slow me down.

Looking back now, part of me regrets it, but at the same time, I recognise that it was an important part of my learning and growth. I simply didn't have the insight into why I was doing the things I did, and how a different path would serve me better. The only choice I could see that would help me slowdown, was physically moving to another location.

I had seen the movie, *The Secret*, and loved it, but at that time, I interpreted it more as a "magic pill" which would change my life ... some day. The concept of putting in the work was a completely foreign idea, and I unconsciously waited for my new, more grown-up life to drop into my lap, at some stage in the future, when I was ready for it.

Maybe that's the point of those decades in our development.

With a bit less hair and a few more wrinkles, our perspective changes. You can truly focus, get locked-in, and enjoy incredible growth that may not have been feasible for you when you were younger.

Whether you're 20-something, or over 70, I truly believe there's still time to make it happen. The foundation to change is to for you to get locked-into what drives you, discover your passion and what you're good at, and start to build a "worthy ideal" that you can strive to. When you go through the process of replacing non-productive paradigms with positive ones, you can truly have the life you've always imagined!

Are you ready to go?

Journal page

> *"You are never too old to set another goal or to dream a new dream."* C S Lewis

- Have you felt as though you missed the boat of success? If yes, what was it that made you feel that way?

- What are some of the limitations that have slowed you down or stopped you in the past?

- What lessons have you learned years ago that will help now?

- Now that you know it's possible for you to have true success, what are some of the actions you feel that could help? What changes will ensure your success?

- Have you used a mentor/coach before? If yes, how did it go? If no, my advice is to find one. What areas of your life and business do you think a great mentor could help you with?

- Many highly successful people have found it at an older age. If you're older than you imagined you would be when you reached your desired level of 'success', (like me), what does success look like for you? How important is it?

- What can you do today to get the wheels in motion?

Age Is No Barrier

Super-Charged Freedom

Belief

What it means to me

A gentleman was walking through an elephant camp, and he spotted that the elephants weren't being kept in cages or held by the use of chains. All that was holding them back was a small piece of rope tied to one of their legs.

As the man gazed upon the elephants, he was completely confused as to why the elephants didn't just use their strength to break the rope and escape the camp. They could easily have done so, yet they didn't even try.

Curious and wanting to know the answer, he asked a trainer nearby why the elephants were just standing there and never tried to escape.

"When they are very young and much smaller, we use the same size rope to tie them, and at that age it's enough to hold them. As they grow up, they are conditioned to believe they cannot break away. They believe the rope can still hold them, so they never try to break free."

The only reason that the elephants weren't breaking free and escaping from the camp was that, over time, they adopted the belief that it just wasn't possible.

The word 'belief' means everything to me. Beliefs form the foundation of our world. Without belief in what you're working towards, you simply will not manifest it into your life. "I'll believe it when I see it," is the age-old phrase we're conditioned to say. I've since learned a different way.

You'll see it, when you believe it.

Our subconscious mind is the mental storehouse of our beliefs. In fact, paradigms are beliefs. That's why we repeatedly attract things into our life that we don't actually want. Sometimes they're false beliefs that we accepted as children, and other times they're beliefs we've created along the way.

One example is related to sleep. We've all heard the expression, "The early bird catches the worm." But how early is early? What time are you getting up? I have gotten out of bed at 5 or 6am for years, to go to the gym. A few months ago, I read Hal Elrod's book, *The Miracle Morning*. An eye-opener in many regards, one of the points Hal makes is that when we go to bed, we set the intention for how we'll wake up. If we believe we'll wake up tired, cranky, and will need 12 coffees to function, that is indeed what will happen. We may decide to create a new habit and set our alarm for a certain time – in my case I decided on 3.33am – but we're thinking, "Oh man, I'll need a massive coffee tomorrow." In that moment, we are creating the belief that we will wake up tired, and your mind will deliver the exact situation you created.

When I switched that belief and decided that I would wake up refreshed and energetic, ready to go through my new morning routine of feeling gratitude, sending love, writing and journaling, and meditating; everything changed. I do wake up feeling full of life and energy. I jump out of bed without a backwards glance, ready to dominate the day.

It all comes down to what we believe. And what we believe dictates our actions, and our actions create our results.

So yes, BELIEF is my favourite word.

The most important ingredient

I poured in the milk and started whisking away with my fork. The two eggs I cracked into the bowl were completely mixed in, making a nice orangey-white colour. I added some chilli flakes and keep stirring. I like a little spice in my scrambled eggs.

Now this is a very simple thing to create, yet there's an order to it. Most recipes require order; "do this, add that, make sure you've done that before this, etc."

My point is that *belief* is an important ingredient in your recipe, but it's not the only ingredient. Without all the things done in a certain way, it will simply be a wish or a hope, not a success plan. You need desire, awareness of your productive and non-productive behaviours, belief that what you want is possible, the ability to make quick decisions to respond to opportunities, and flexibility to change direction in the pursuit of your goal.

In Chapter 1, you made a list of what you want. I asked you to get really specific and also to dream big. The beauty of this is that you're really using that magical part of your mind, imagination.

This word "belief" is going to truly allow you to work like a magician and pull you towards what you truly desire. Sounds easy, right? Yes, sometimes it can be. What you're seeking, is also seeking you. However, when those tricky paradigms are at play, the ones you've got programmed that have you feeling less than worthy or not quite as good as Daryl Bloggs down the road, you'll find that getting your mind to BELIEVE is a bit harder. That's where you'll need to reprogram it.

Bob (Proctor) recommends that when you decide the new paradigm or program you want to run, write it out 100 times in the morning and 100 times at night and watch what happens. It won't be long until you're starting to feel how you need to feel to get into a "belief state".

Start writing down some of your "non-productive actions/behaviours" and decide on one or two that you want to change, so you can start to build more belief in your dream.

It's a recipe you can design. Go on, start now!

How do we create it?

The Power of Awareness by Neville Goddard truly nails the ideas behind belief. He teaches how to go beyond your imagination, and truly conjure the *feeling* of already having what you desire. Not how it will feel when you get there. But how it feels right now to already be there.

Can you get yourself into this state? The more you can do it and really visualise and "feel" how it feels, smell the scents, almost touch certain parts, you will create that belief, and in turn, you will manifest what you desire super-fast. You will experience the quantum leap that people talk about.

After years of personal development and believing in the Law of Attraction and manifestation, I still suffered through many bouts of doubt and questioning. *Will I ever really make this happen? Is this just a pipe dream? Am I setting myself up for disappointment?*

When I read Goddard's take on attracting your desires, it flipped a switch for me. I went from dabbling in this practice to taking it on as my natural state. I used my imagination to feel into desired situations on a regular basis; to the point that I intentionally blurred the lines between current events and imagined ones.

At the time I first read this book, I was working with a couple of clients who were not putting in the work required to achieve the transformation they had come to me for. Both wanted to quit the program, deciding it was "too hard" to get what they desired.

"I can't see how this is going to work for me," Dan had said, looking at the floor during our video call. "It obviously works for others, but I guess a loser like me is never going to get what I want."

My conversation with Jacob was similar.

I knew it wasn't the case for either man, and despite using my coaching skills and tools to support them, they both appeared to be falling into a deeper, darker hole in every call.

As a committed coach, I didn't take it upon myself to be attached to or responsible for their outcomes, but I equally did not want to let them off the hook. I wanted to see these men achieve their greatest dreams. After all, that was my role as their mentor.

Having just read Goddard's book, I was inspired to change my own approach. Throughout the day, when that familiar threat of overwhelm would creep into my conscious thought, I would immediately interrupt that program and replace it with my new, desired state. I imagined the way I wanted the calls to go. I pictured my clients smiling, happy, and eager to move forward. I thanked the universe for giving me this opportunity for contrast.

"While I don't want to continue to coach this type of client, I am grateful for the experience, and this is how I see Dan and Jacob feeling about themselves moving forward – doing the work, getting into the right mindset, and accomplishing insane results," I would say, while closing my eyes and feeling the immense glow of satisfaction I knew I would feel when it happened as I had pictured it.

At that time, although I had experienced the Law of Attraction in other areas of my life, where I was the person who was directly impacted on, or had to make changes, the idea of being able to influence the outcome for others felt beyond my grasp. A small part of me held an element of doubt beneath the surface of my confidence.

But I knew it was possible. I'd seen it for myself, and I'd seen it many times in others, especially within the mentoring group I was a part of. So, I trusted, and I believed. I really, really believed.

Within days, the scenario with both men changed dramatically. The conversations I had with them so closely resembled the ones I had imagined that it was almost scary. Some of the details I had envisaged, such as the wording they would use when they decided to stick with my program, manifested with uncanny accuracy.

"Brett, you were right," Jacob said, grinning at me from across the pond. "I'm so glad you didn't give up on me. I know this is going to work and I'm already feeling the change."

That's the power of belief.

The power of belief

You've decided what you want. You've set a goal. You know you're going to achieve it.

Or perhaps you're like I was, currently stuck on that last one.

Why? Because you don't truly believe yet, and are saying to yourself, "I'll believe it when I see it."

Despite this being a saying we've heard by everyone from our granddad to our colleagues, it's completely backwards.

You must *believe* first, in order to see it.

We MUST reprogram our minds to get into the state of belief. If you're disconnected from what you consciously think you want, it's almost guaranteed to be due to non-belief.

That's why I put so much value into this word, and so should you.

Just recently I found new meaning in the famous quote by Denis Waitley. I had spent around two years hearing this quote and never quite understood how it applied to me.

"It's not who you are that holds you back, it's who you think you're not!"

I had been invited to be part of an amazing Men's Summit and was working closely with an inspirational group of successful men. Every speaker was asked to share a story that would be relatable to the audience and had a theme of what it meant to be a man.

While I was preparing for the event, I happened to read this quote again. But this time, I saw it differently. I felt a strong need to dig deeper into this quote and find its meaning in my life.

I suddenly saw it very differently. It's crazy to think you can hear something over and over again and then finally, when you dig for the answer by asking questions, it simply "unfolds".

People always looked at me as a non-typical male, and subsequently I looked at myself that way. I had grown up with predominately all-female influences – my mother, grandmother, two aunties, and I had no father figure or male role model in my life. I felt deeply connected to my feminine and particularly with my wardrobe of bright colours and flowery shirts, I appeared as far from a beer-swilling Aussie bloke as you can get. I didn't get into fights, and I found it easy to talk to women.

However, on closer inspection of my years of self-sabotage and not living or speaking my truth, I had an epiphany.

Holy shit, I realised. *I am just about as "typical male" as they come.*

- I didn't show my feelings at all (I hadn't cried as an adult until the financial incident I mentioned at the start of the book).
- I was only fully honest when it suited me.
- I always thought I could fix situations myself because I was a "strong" man.
- I never asked for help. Looking back, I had many opportunities to change my situation by doing this, but was blinded by my own ego.

Despite appearances to the contrary, internally (where it matters) I was definitely using all the personality traits/ behaviour that were attached to some poor self-beliefs. It wasn't conscious – these behaviours and habits were simply effects of the root cause, which was my belief. I had a damaged self-belief and lack of self-worth, and I didn't acknowledge that until I shone a light on it in 2018, when I started truly doing the work on myself.

Once you get the awareness of what's wrong or not working, decide to take action and find a way to reprogram it without quitting, you're guaranteed to start seeing dramatic changes in your life, just as I did.

Journal page

> *"Success is often achieved by those who don't know that failure is inevitable."*
> *Coco Chanel*

- This was the most important change I needed to make. What beliefs or behaviours do you recognise that are not serving you?

- What are 1 or 2 scenarios in your life that you feel you failed in and what could you have done differently to change the outcome?

- Which beliefs do you possess that you instinctively know are holding you back, and why?

- To manually change a belief/behaviour, we need to write out a positive (opposite) of the current belief/program running and start affirming it with feeling, as if we've already achieved it. Write on one sheet of paper the way you currently operate (negative or non-productive) and on another sheet, the positive/preferred. Focus on doing one of these (starting with the most important) for 30 days or until you see the change in your results.

- I mentioned that in order for affirmations to be effective, we have to get into the feeling "as if we already possess", however I know some people have trouble imagining something they've never done. So, ask yourself some deep questions. What could one or two of them be?

- There is a quote "it's not who you think you are that holds you back, it's who you think you're not that does." How does this relate to you?

- If you could wave a magic wand and fix any belief/behaviour, which ones do you believe would have the most significance in your transformation?

Belief

Super-Charged Freedom

Guidance

My decision to get help

In the movie *The Matrix*, Neo finally realises that he's living in a simulated reality and Morpheus trains him to become "The One", harnessing his special skills to bring peace to the Matrix.

As someone who didn't ask for help for most of my life, the message in this movie has a lot of significance for me.

I went through years thinking that I could sort things out on my own. I didn't need anyone's advice or guidance. I was certainly keen on being successful and making money, but I didn't truly invest. I didn't go to the next level of implementing and mastering, and of making the lessons I was presented with part of my life. Not surprisingly, when I did read a book or listen to a podcast, I didn't take the required actions and didn't move the needle much in my life as a result.

In November 2018, when I finally had my epiphany that I was going to be successful in my own way, I knew it was time to truly plant, water, and nurture my seed of success. I knew I had to stop trying to figure it out alone and stop thinking that I had the knowledge I needed. After all, my financial dire straits and general life situation was evidence that I hadn't mastered all that I learned and read about.

Once I made the decision to get help, I just had to find the right person to guide me. This is exactly the time I was contacted on Instagram by Marcus, the young guy I mentioned in an earlier chapter. He then introduced me to Mariko, who became my coach and was the catalyst to my first tastes of genuine success.

At this stage, I didn't even have savings to get started, but Mariko gave me a few tips to manifest the deposit I required to get started, and two days later it was green lights. When you're truly, subconsciously, connected to the reality you want, magic starts to happen.

From that point on, it wasn't all smooth sailing and, the truth is, when you decide to engage help and learn and apply the necessary skills to succeed, it's confronting. You often need to stop some bad behaviours and paradigms, and when I say stop, I mean swap. Because if you simply stop a negative paradigm without replacing its polar opposite, often a new negative will take its place.

In the few years since, my life has changed dramatically. With the help of numerous mentors and coaches, I'm now thriving in most areas of my life.

Bob Proctor is my ultimate guide and mentor for changing my paradigms and beliefs; James Whittaker (author of *Think and Grow Rich: The Legacy* and co-producer of the movie with the same name) is my performance coach; Cathryn Mora (director of Change Empire Books) is my book coach; David Meltzer is my business coach; as well as other coaches for my health, fitness, and general wellbeing.

In each one of those areas, I've had unprecedented progress and growth, and I know unequivocally that I wouldn't have reached these outcomes alone.

Ultimately, when you need help because things aren't working the way you'd like, stop and decide if you would benefit from a guide in the area you're struggling. It will be the ticket to the fast train, overriding your unicycle.

Bob Proctor's journey

Bob tells the story of when he decided to start his journey, he was earning $4,000 per year and owed $6,000. *That's not a big deal*, I thought at the time, then immediately concluded that it was much like saying you earn $40,000 per year and owe $60,000. The fact he could come out of that and reach such a prosperous place within a relatively short amount of time is incredibly impressive. But this wasn't the part of the story that sold me on Bob.

The part that truly resonated with me was the action he took and the results he got after his first mentor, Ray Stanford, had suggested that Bob read *Think and Grow Rich* by Napoleon Hill. He said, "Bob, if you read and follow the instructions in this book, you'll get rich," and Bob's response was, "I can't read." It wasn't quite true – Bob could read – but he hadn't read much since school.

Bob asked Ray why this book was so important and how he knew it could work for him. Ray replied by asking Bob these questions, "Have you ever seen me without money?" and Bob replied, "No." He then asked, "Have you ever seen me sick?" and again Bob replied, "No." Finally, he said, "Do you ever see me unhappy?" and, of course, Bob had never seen Ray unhappy at all. Then Ray went on to say, "Bob, whenever I see you, you're asking someone for a couple of bucks. You never have money. You often have a cold or look unwell, and many times I've seen you quite depressed," and Bob agreed with these statements, as confronting as they were.

Ray said, "This book will find you happy, healthy, and wealthy, just like me. However, there's one important key to ensuring this will work for you."

Bob asked, "What's that?"

"You MUST have discipline."

Bob read *Think and Grow Rich* religiously. He wrote down on a card that he wanted to earn $25,000 for the year, which in 1961, with his previous track record this was a ludicrous idea. He kept working on his affirmation of the goal and when that year ended, he actually earned over $100,000. In the following few years, he earned over $1,000,000.

So how did he make the money? He came up with an idea. *Why don't I start a cleaning business? I'll clean floors; I'm not proud,* he thought. He started the business in Toronto and grew it into a multi-national company with offices in Canada, the United States, and England.

Bob recalls that at one point, he wondered how on earth he had really achieved those heights. He had virtually no schooling and no business experience, but was eager to learn more. He'd been listening to Earl Nightingale's record, *The Strangest Secret* for a while, and wondered if he could work with him? Earl and his business partner, Lloyd Conant, were pioneers in teaching people personal development, and their business was very successful. He approached them for a low-paying job so that he could observe their practice, and Lloyd introduced Bob to a little green book called *The Science of Getting Rich* by Wallace D. Wattles. This was Bob's next "all-in" program, and after five years of working with Earl and Lloyd, Bob decided to start his own business.

That "little green book" was also the inspiration for Rhonda Byrne in creating the hit movie *The Secret*.

Finding your own mentor

"I don't want to pay someone to help me ... I don't have the money ... What if I don't get anything out of it?"

These are the things I said to myself multiple times over the years. I worried that investing in a coach or mentor was out of my reach. It felt like a risk, and I decided that doing it myself was the best option.

Looking back, this was a key factor to me not fully reaching my goals and achieving my dreams. I would achieve a certain level of success and then back away from them or not go all the way. Something was often getting in my way, but it wasn't obvious what that was.

Once I invested in coaches, everything changed. I realised that my aversion to getting and paying for support was a barrier to my success.

If you're like I was, or most people who come to me for coaching, you know what you want and you have goals, but at some point along the way, worry, doubt, and fear kick in and override your ability to move in that direction.

Make the decision now to invest in a coach or mentor for an area which is important to you. If you want to reach new heights in your life, relationship, and business or career, find someone you resonate with, someone who inspires you. Their words and energy need to really make you feel something special.

Getting referrals is valuable, but go beyond this and do your own research. Talk to prospective coaches or mentors and see if you are a good fit for each other. This is important, because when you trust in someone to help you, you need to know that you like them and also that they've got the necessary experience to help you.

A great coach WILL NOT give up on you. Even if you piss them off. A great coach or mentor does what's required to help you grow, and growth isn't always "sunshine and rainbows", otherwise everyone would be winning.

Search online, make a shortlist, go to some seminars, workshops, watch their videos on YouTube or organise a Discovery session. Take some time to work out who feels right for you. But then GO! Take ACTION as soon as you can. Why? Because making a quick decision is one of the common denominators of success. Some of the most successful people make quick (calculated) decisions and rarely change their mind, if ever. The opposite to this (which I was) is taking loads of time to decide and changing your mind frequently.

Do your research and then DECIDE!

Masterminding

If you already have the support of a coach/mentor, a mastermind adds another important realm to the manifestation of your dreams and desires. Masterminding with people with the right intention and order will help you dramatically. As an individual we "know what we know", and only have our own experiences to search through when making decisions.

In addition to having the influence of experienced people, being in a mastermind offers great accountability. If you say you're going to do something and you return the following week, you want to be able to say you did it.

Who you mastermind *with* is crucial. Make sure everyone is fully committed to positive change and growth. If you choose a few people (no more than 8–10) and one of them is out of harmony, it will totally disrupt the power of the mastermind.

Choose carefully. Try to find people who are quite different from you, or who have more success. If you truly want to grow, you need the right people. As the saying goes, "If you're the smartest person in the room, you're in the wrong room."

Napoleon Hill mentions in *The Power of the Mastermind* that even Andrew Carnegie (richest man in the world in the early 1900s) owed much of his triumph to masterminding with other successful people. Henry Ford and Thomas A. Edison did it too. In fact, many of the current world's thought leaders, including Bob Proctor and Tony Robbins, owe some of their achievements to masterminding.

Can you think of some people you could do this with starting next week? Even start with one or two. Just start!

Journal page

> *"You just have to have the guidance to lead you in the direction until you can do it yourself."* Tina Yothers

- Have you decided to get help from a coach/mentor? If so, why?
- What sort of help do you feel you need? List some of the benefits.
- Have you considered who could be a good mentor/coach for you and why?
- Who has been a good mentor for you so far, and why?
- If you were giving others guidance, what would be one or two pieces of advice you feel could help someone in business or life in general?
- Start listing some people you could mastermind with.
- What do you believe the benefits of masterminding will be for you?

Guidance

Super-Charged Freedom

Abundance

A lack of money isn't the problem

Most men who to come to me for coaching want to earn more money. They believe that with more money, they'll be happier, more fulfilled, more confident, and it will give them more stability. Beyond that, there are perceived societal expectations and the ability or lack thereof to fulfil their role as a provider.

Some men think it's just about *how* to earn more money. They want me to teach them what to do to make more money; to show them what I'm doing or help them discover ways to bring in more income.

Other men have insight a little beyond this. They do realise that it's not really about the "how" or the "doing" – they know a mindset shift will be required to reach their financial goals, but they're still looking outside themselves. They think there is something they're not seeing, and by working with me, they will suddenly discover the secret. They want me to simply point them in the right direction and after that, the money will flow.

Remember, these men are smart, capable, hardworking men. There is nothing "wrong" with someone just because their bank balance isn't currently reflecting the abilities they know they have. Equally, there is nothing wrong with asking for help.

And in a way, it is a simple mindset shift, but at the same time, it's so much more than that.

The issue here is that so many men – so many people – are still looking *outside themselves* for the key. That if they just tweak something they're doing, something they're not doing, or approach it with a different attitude, that all their problems will be solved, and money will no longer be an issue.

Their focus is on what they don't have and how they're limited in some way. They blame situations or other people – or the world around them. What kind of job they have, what they're doing in their career or business, where they live, what they look like. These are external factors, and while they can contribute to our financial situation, they are not why we got there, and changing them won't make any difference if we don't go deeper.

They will say things like, "I would love to earn more money, but I'm already earning in the top bracket of my industry," "I'd love to earn more, but that would mean getting another qualification or learning something new, and I don't have the time for that with the kids and everything else ..." or "I definitely want to make more money, but first I have to focus on paying off some debt ..."

Do any of these sound familiar? Have you said something similar to yourself or someone else?

Don't worry, you're not alone.

Ultimately, all these things are excuses – but when we say them to ourselves (or others), we believe that they are facts. They *feel* like legitimate reasons, but in reality, everything is changeable.

Even when men are ready for coaching, it's usually not going to be the journey they think it will be. They *will* earn more, but not by doing what they think they need to do.

Delving into your own money story will unearth a whole range of limitations you didn't even know you had been placing on yourself.

My client Brendan came to me in a place of severe financial struggle. His wife was the primary breadwinner, as his income was totally erratic and mostly very low. Brendan felt like the key to his success lay just around the corner with the next idea, the next qualification, the next course. Nothing he tried or invested in seemed to achieve its full potential, and he was beyond frustrated.

Brendan was from a middle-class American family with strong family values. He felt like he was letting down his wife and children by not earning more. He was driven by the need to provide and to "be a man". He was so focused on the "things", the external factors, and "how" to best achieve his goals (which vehicle, which program, which qualification). He hadn't examined what was going on for him at a deeper level.

When Brendan started working with me, I could feel his frustration deeply. I recognised it in myself, and how I had previously operated in my own marriage and life. I knew that if Brendan was anything like me, he'd need to have quiet time, and to go deeper, to ask the universe for what he wanted, and then be open to receiving.

"Brendan, I want you to take half an hour of quiet time every day this week," I said. "I just want you to quiet your mind. Don't think about the current situations or circumstances, and just allow any positive guidance or ideas to come to you. Take note of them, but it's not about you doing something. It's about just being with yourself."

He wasn't giving himself any mental space to breathe, and to allow ideas and thoughts to come to him. He was too busy trying to control everything that was happening outside and gave no energy to the inside.

Our conscious mind is reported to operate at 40 bits per second (bps), in comparison with our subconscious mind, which races ahead at 40,000,000 bps. Trying to control your outcomes by addressing exterior forces using your conscious brain, or your "will", is much like trying to break into a government agency's computer mainframe using your Nintendo. It's powerless to achieve the outcome you desire.

Working with me for a few months, Brendan finally realised he had been fighting the wrong battle.

He let go of trying to physically make things happen. He stopped trying to control things. Instead, he started quietening his mind. He listened to his inner voice and became open to receive. He reprogrammed the old, unhelpful paradigms which had not been serving him, by writing down his goals, repeating affirmations, and really feeling into the life he wanted.

A couple of key people came into his life who created new and exciting opportunities for him in his previously flailing business, and then new ideas seemed to crop up out of nowhere, which created even more opportunities. He also took action because he felt inspired, rather than because he was desperate.

None of this is coincidence, as this is how the Universal Laws operate.

Your money patterns

How did you get where you are now?

First, let's look at your earnings history. What do you currently earn or what's the most you've ever earned in a year?

Look back over the past 5 to 10 years, write down those figures, and then average it out ... Are there any obvious patterns in your earnings related to the average? Namely, have you ever had a year where you earned, say, $100k, and in the previous year, you earned $50k and then had an adjustment the following year, so that really, your average was closer to $75k? I did. In 2006, I earned $50k, 2007 was close to $100k, and 2008 dropped back to $75k. I convinced myself it was because of the Global Financial Crisis and moving cities, but my income had been erratic for years.

These earning patterns are not really to do with the money itself. We have to think about money as an energy, not the paper it's printed on or the gold coins that represent it. The higher your energy is around your own self-worth, the higher your stock goes up; when you internally have a higher view of yourself, you can earn more money and live a better life.

Get clear on why you want more

Get clear on your "why". Why do you want to earn more money? What does it mean to you? What will more money create in your life? What will it give you?

If your answer was something like, "a Porsche," or "a new house", or "regular holidays", then dig deeper. If you had those things, how do you think you'd feel?

Happier, more confident, more free ...?

Create a vision of what money means to you and what you believe it will bring you.

When Jonathan started working with me, he had a goal of earning $10 million a year. He'd been dreaming about it for years and with his salary in the five-figure range, he was far, far from this goal. When speaking about his current progress towards his goal, I could see the deflation written all over his body.

The next question I asked him was, "What does $10 million represent for you?"

Jonathan's eyes immediately lit up. "It would mean we'd have no mortgage, we'd have savings, we'd be able to invest in property, and be able to easily pay for our children's education."

With that response, I could see that he was already a step closer to achieving his goal.

Jonathan had been really focused on his goal, which was great, and had started various businesses to achieve the goal, but hadn't really connected with what this money would bring him. Besides that, his businesses had "failed", and he hadn't forgiven himself for putting his family through the financial and emotional stress of his near-bankruptcy. So, there was also a lot of emotional turmoil wrapped up in his financial situation.

The key to moving towards new goals is getting clear on why you want this goal and what it would mean to you.

Millionaire traits

When you are clear on why you want more money, how do you bridge the gap?

When you think about it, you got to where you are because of a certain set of beliefs and resultant actions.

"What got you here will not get you there," Abraham Hicks is famous for saying.

In order to reach an amount of money or achieve a lifestyle you've never had, you need to be prepared to approach things differently, and essentially "be" a different person. The key is to identify as someone who earns that much. You need to think and act like someone who is a $10 million earner (or however much you want). You must adopt the habits of someone who does earn that much and get into the mindset of someone who is already there.

What characteristics does a millionaire typically have?

This answer is many and varied, but generally they will get out of bed early; they work on their mind and goals first thing in the morning by doing affirmations, journaling, goal setting, and practising gratitude. They will also usually workout or move their body in some way.

Millionaires are often, although not always, focused and disciplined. If they make the decision to do something, they will stick to their word – not just to others, but to themselves.

More than likely, a millionaire with a successful business will be positive and happy. Not false, pretend happy, but more focused on things that make them feel good and bring about positive results, rather than focusing on what doesn't work, and what makes them feel bad, stressed, or worried.

Of course, there are always moments and situations where you'll immediately react by feeling bad, but it must be temporary. Your overall mindset and focus need to be more on what makes you feel good, what is going right, and what you can learn from any situation in order to progress and grow.

"Feeling the feelings" is key to the universal Law of Attraction. It means conjuring up the feeling of happiness (or abundance, or confidence, or whatever you seek) from any situation or thought that you can. The more you feel a certain way, the more you will bring situations towards you that create those same feelings.

One of the hardest things at first can be to feel the way you want to feel, based on your goals and desires, rather than constantly feeling based on what currently IS. When you keep your energy focused on what IS, rather than what you WANT, you get more of what is.

Therefore, in order to start feeling the way you want to feel, earning the money you'd like to earn, and reaching the success you'd like to reach, you need to start with exploring what's happening on the inside and then shift your thoughts and actions accordingly.

In Jonathan's case, connecting with his why enabled him to think creatively about how to achieve his $10 million goal.

He came up with a consultancy business based on his decades of experience in customer service. He narrowed down to a niche where the market wasn't competitive for his ideal clients, and customer service would set them apart. Aware of the difference it could make, businesses were prepared to invest heavily in Jonathan's support.

A year later, his business, and his finances, are flourishing; and it's only the beginning. Jonathan has plans for licensing his system and expansion is on the cards.

"I can't afford it"

Another common hurdle in the path of achieving our goals is saying that you can't afford things.

The first time I spoke to a sales consultant from the Proctor Gallagher Institute, I was excited to hear about the 13-month Bob Proctor Coaching Program.

Of course, the first question I asked was, "How much is it?".

"$10,000," he said.

My heart sank because I knew it was out of my reach. "Oh mate, there's no way I can afford that," I said.

He suggested an alternate program for $440, which was exactly the amount I had saved. I signed up.

A couple of years later, when I had progressed in leaps and bounds in my life and business, I became the person on the other side of the phone.

Jack was a client who abandoned his program, and hadn't finished paying it off either. However, I saw great potential in him, and reminded myself of why I became a coach in the first place, and how I was here to serve others. I had made the commitment to never give up.

A few months after he'd left my program, I spoke to Jack to check in and see how he was travelling and to offer a discussion about joining one of my new mastermind client groups. His first response was, "Thanks for reaching out. I can't afford to do that. I have to buy a new car and I've got kids' schooling to consider. I'm on a strict budget."

I recognised that response from myself in years gone by, always using my current reality and sets of conditions as to why I couldn't possibly consider doing "this" or "that.

Hearing this response and considering the types of clients I admit to these groups, I thanked Jack for his response and said, "No problem, Jack. I hear what you're saying and I can appreciate it because I've been there myself. However, at the moment, you're only looking at it based on your current reality, and making your decision based on what you can or can't do today, rather than making your decision on what you *want* to do. The more you keep accepting your current reality about why you can't do something, the longer you're going to stay there. So, the decision you need to make today is whether you're prepared to be open to looking at a new way to move forward, or to simply say no and just accept the current reality the way it is."

Several of my other clients had been in similar financial situations when they joined me, but had been ready to receive significant change and were open to looking for ways to make it happen. They found financial support where they could, and invested in themselves and their desired future. Taking the action inspired more action and the subsequent change. I could tell from Jack's response that he wasn't ready yet.

Jack mulled it over for a few moments. "I see what you're saying, and I do want to change my situation. What do I need to do?" he said.

"You need to make the decision that you want to do it, and then find a way to make it happen. I suggest you read Chapter 3 of *Think and Grow Rich*, which is about faith. Then write out an affirmation along the lines of, "I am so happy and grateful now that I have the money to be in Brett's mastermind group, and am working towards my goals."

I didn't want to push Jack to join if it wasn't the right move for him. But I did want him to see the ways he was limiting himself, and keeping himself exactly where he was already stuck.

Jack joined the group.

The transformation was incredible. Jack upped the ante and made the decision to pay his program ahead of schedule. Money started flowing to him from his side business, from foundations he'd put in place previously but hadn't materialised yet; and within a month, he paid off the program in full.

The key is in making your decisions based on what you want, not what currently is. Where you are now is a sum of all the decisions and actions you've taken up until now. If you want something different, you must do something different.

Other common blocks and pitfalls

My poor relationship with money was perhaps my biggest downfall. I partially attribute this to the habits of the role models available in my life (and the role models of my role models before them), and it was also a matter of developing poor money habits of my own.

I always wanted that next best thing, and it started to become more of a coping mechanism for the other aspects of myself that weren't working. Bob Proctor says there is a direct correlation between your relationship with money and your self-image or how you feel about yourself. My image was very poor. I had an unhealthy obsession with getting rid of money as quickly as possible.

When I was in real estate, I was offered a phenomenal deal on a townhouse in Brighton (Melbourne) Australia. It's one of the wealthiest areas of Melbourne, right near the beach, and it was where I worked and sold property. My wife and I put a deposit down and applied for a loan. After anxiously waiting the few days it took to get a response, we were really disappointed to hear that the loan wasn't approved.

"Elissa, let's go to Dunk Island for a holiday," I said, five minutes after hanging up the phone to the bank officer.

Elissa looked up from her coffee, her brow furrowed in confusion. "What? Shouldn't we try and sort out the loan first?"

What I hadn't told her was that our knockback was certainly the result of my very poor credit history. Because I was in the habit of concealing some of the deeper truths from my wife, she knew I'd had some money issues, but not how deeply they ran.

"Oh, I think the universe is showing us that it's not the right house. Maybe we need to step back for a while and see what happens," I said, immediately deflecting my focus away from our financial strife. They were returning our deposit, and I needed to spend it.

I didn't want to face the truth about my situation. I had feigned optimism when applying for the loan, but now the gig was up. There was clearly no point in me addressing or facing my issues, and I didn't even realise I was avoiding it. Everything about money was short-term for me. I wouldn't have a shiny new house to focus on, so I needed another fix.

Did I know the value of a long-term strategy? Hell, yes. But I was hypnotised by my spending spree mentality – always looking for short-term satisfaction. Buying "things", going out drinking, partying, never truly focused on a strategy for the future.

My wife was much more sensible and future focused. She had great ideas and the personality and commitment to implement them, but I was good at distracting her, or at times, simply lying to her. She never truly knew the depth of my distraction*.

(*Elissa was a truly great wife and even better friend. I'm lucky I've repaired or restored part of that trust back with her since our son Orlando was born. It took me a solid few years, but I got there and was grateful to have made our friendship work, as I'm positive it helps my son having that sort of stability between two parents.)

If we only examine our spending decisions, we're only treating the effect. We're not looking at the underlying cause. Our money habits don't come from nowhere.

Our childhood role models do have an initial part to play, although this isn't about blame. Looking back at my childhood, I had to forgive both the adults in my life, and myself. I also had to let go of some stories in order to see the effects dissipate when it came to spending money.

Growing up, my mum moved us around a lot. I went to seven different primary schools. We never had a lot of money, but my mum always made sure I had what I wanted. We lived by the principle of surviving week to week and getting a treat on special occasions. Perhaps that's where part of it stemmed. I also recognise not having my dad or a father figure impacted me, especially as a teenager. I was a great candidate for juvenile detention with my shoplifting, breaking and entering, graffiti, and stealing cars, and I often felt a yearning for that male influence. Every time I would reach out to my dad, I wouldn't get what I was hoping for.

I had to forgive my dad, my mum, and myself, for the past. While those many crazy and sometimes outrageous and dangerous experiences have made me what I am today, it doesn't mean I want to repeat them.

In addition to the money stories I dismantled, there were other benefits I realised from my past. My dad was not present in my life, and through this, he actually gave me a gift unknowingly. He wasn't equipped to be a hands-on father, and by not being there, he created a desire in me to be an amazing inspiration to my own son. I believe I've been doing that from the day he was born and I'm not slowing down.

The point of talking about the past is simply to recognise that we all have a history. Who we are today is a sum of that history, but we don't want to carry it around forever. You need the awareness of what's not working in your life, and what isn't serving you; and then it's time to go through a process of recognising where it came from, forgiving yourself and others, and then moving through it. It's like unblocking yourself and allowing yourself to break free from your old stories.

Take the time to look back and ask yourself ...

"Am I holding on to crap that doesn't serve me?"

Creating a new self-image

Most of us are going through life wanting to be happy. We are looking for things on the outside which we believe will make us happy. It will never happen, or at least not to the depth we want it to. The truth is that true happiness comes from the inside. It's from loving ourselves unconditionally and accepting ourselves that we can begin to find what we need – from within.

How do we know where we're lacking in our self-image, and what do we need to do in order to change it?

Ask yourself these questions and carefully consider your answers. You may want to write them down.

What is some of the negative self-talk you're engaging in?

Do you say things to yourself like, *I'm not good enough ... I'm not as young and energetic as I used to be ... I'm not smart enough ... I'm too ... I can't do this because ...*

The more you focus on what you don't want or what you don't have, you will stay in lack. You are reinforcing what you don't want to think, feel, or do, and giving yourself more of the same. You can't get to a place of abundance from here. The Laws of Attraction and Vibration say that you can't make a huge jump – from complete negativity to overwhelming positivity – but what you can do is slightly improve your thinking, one step at a time.

You receive a phone call from the bank and someone has spent $3,000 of your savings, yet that was this months bill payments and the bank doesn't know when they'll get the return of funds, as it can't yet be proven as stolen. You start to spiral into depression. "I'm going to receive a default on my credit history." "I don't have anymore income for another month, how will I eat." "I can't borrow from anyone and my credit cards are maxed, probably gonna get kicked out of our rental."

These feelings are natural, but they are absolutely unhelpful. So how do we change the inner dialogue? First of all it starts with the awareness that you can change your situation. Next step is to start focusing on how it feels to have this problem resolved quickly. How does it make you feel getting another call from the bank stating "Mr Scott, we have great news. Video footage of a woman using your card has been sourced and the police know who she is. We have updated your account with the $3,000" Do you feel elation? Relief? Which bill do you pay first? It's a satisfying feeling right?

Lastly, it's writing out ideas of how you could possibly solve the situation. But not necessarily how 'YOU' would do it. Look at this issue from someone else's point of view. What would Tony Robbins do in this situation, not taking into account his current lifestyle and back balance, his personality. What ideas do you think Tony might have? Or perhaps someone like Henry Ford. He was well known for having a desk with push buttons attached, each button would call to an employee who would come in and answer any question he had. After all, Henry barely attended school at all.

Focus on solutions. Always know, there is often a way to change the situation and it doesn't start by picking up the phone or going straight into action. Often I've fixed situation simply by increasing my mood, but taking myself for a walk in nature. Raising my vibration has completely solved situations for me, more than a few times.

Do you lack energy or enthusiasm for things you used to enjoy?

If so, when you think about it, where does that come from? I used to identify as a major extrovert, yet over the years I increasingly disliked crowds, parties, or any social event. I dismissed it as just getting older and becoming more introverted. Looking back, I know that it was just me "showing up", unconsciously putting on a mask and looking happy and bright. It was a way of avoiding people seeing the real me – the me who had no idea what I was doing and how to get out of the rollercoaster shit storm I'd been living in.

Have you experienced a big change in personality or habits?

Do you love what you do, or do you hate it?

If you feel drained and frustrated by your daily activities, whether that be in business or a job, you might think, "Yes, but if I keep going, eventually I'll get the result and then I can move up."

It actually has the opposite effect. Doing work which drains or frustrates you will cause more angst, stress, and anxiety, and you'll end up burning out and losing energy altogether. It doesn't enable you to make the progress you desire.

There will be "things" you don't enjoy doing, even in your dream business or job, but overall, if you're doing something you truly love doing, your self-belief and self-esteem will skyrocket.

Do you look for validation from others to feel good?

Humans crave interaction, affection, and validation. It's fair to say that all people seek a certain amount of validation from others, although some people are much more evolved in terms of not allowing the opinions or words of others to affect them at a deep level.

Do you crave phrases like, "You're so smart," "You're so handsome," "I couldn't have done this without you," or similar?

Does attention from your romantic partner make you swell with pride, but a lack of it makes you look elsewhere for the same? Do compliments from business partners fuel you to succeed and criticism have you tempted to call quits on the partnership?

Looking for validation from others is an endless and very unsatisfying game. It's human nature to take people for granted, and the saying, "familiarity breeds contempt" is fairly true. The longer somebody is in your life, the less likely they are to feed you with the constant stream of compliments you require to feel appreciated. This means you'll always be chasing the next best person, activity, or venture to fuel your ego.

This is why it's imperative to sustain your own needs by recognising and feeling good about your self-worth.

Do you avoid speaking to groups?

If you're a coach or entrepreneur, do you avoid situations where you need to speak to groups, such as live videos, speaking to others at networking events, or presenting? If so, do you find that you're fine speaking one-on-one?

This can be a sign of low self-confidence, based on a fear of what the group will think of you. In a one-on-one discussion, it's easier to read the body language and reaction of the other person. That can make it more comfortable to speak your mind or share your feelings, without as much concern for how it will be received. In a large group, however, you can't keep track of everybody's reactions or impressions, so dealing with potential reactions can be overwhelming. The bigger the group, the more concerning it can be for people who are lacking in the confidence to just do and say what they feel, regardless.

I'm not saying that you need to disregard what anybody thinks of us, because as humans, most of us still do care a certain degree, but if you have true inner belief and confidence, you can share your message more courageously.

I used to act confident in front of a group, but internally I was suffering. I wasn't aware of my barriers at the time, but I did know that I was feeling fear and I passed it off as a fear of public speaking. Looking back, I was so lacking in self-belief that I was worried how people would see me and what I might say, which would make me look stupid. I was able to put on a brave face, but it was all for show.

Ask yourself these questions:

- How do you remove these barriers?
- How do you go from this to making more money?
- Ask yourself if you're wearing a mask? Is that the "real" you?

- What would happen if you didn't change your self-image?
- Who are some people that have self-images you like? Could you start to "act" like them?
- What is one thing you could implement today to change how you internally view yourself?

Start reading more on topics relating to the Universal Laws and people who've used them to earn more money than they'll ever need. If you're like me, and struggle to keep your attention on a book, go to YouTube, Audible or somewhere else that you can listen to a book or watch a video related to the topic. Look for recommended or popular books and authors, and then see who you feel connected to, so that you can go deeper.

Making money can't be motivated by greed, because the satisfaction is generally short-lived. Make more money so you can help more people. Help your family and friends, help people that you personally would like to help. Share the wealth. Teach others.

Keep learning. One of the other great lessons Bob Proctor teaches is, "There's only two ways to make money." When I first heard this, I thought, *That's not true, I've been offered half a dozen different ways just this week!*

However, he's right.

You're either working for money or money is working for you.

So, when you're ready to start earning the money you truly desire, remember – it's got to be you in charge of money; you're the boss. Choose some strategies or ways you can build your wealth via multiple sources of income, ideally including some passive income streams. I believe most successful people have at least 8 to 10 different ways. That way, if one stops working, you've got backup and the income you "work for" is no longer the revenue you depend upon to pay bills and live.

Money management

After getting through some of my worst financial moments, I decided to hire a financial adviser. At the time I made the decision I wasn't earning much, but I knew that my success was inevitable, and even when you get stronger at earning money, it doesn't always translate into knowing how to look after or grow it. Adam Kennedy of Ethical Financial Advice also became a friend and trusted confidante, and his support and knowledge has highlighted the money areas I used to be completely oblivious to or in denial about.

My advice is to find someone you trust to give you some great advice about understanding budgets, investing money, handling super, and creating a nest egg. Even if you earn ten times the amount of money, you could easily find ten more ways to spend it. Bob Proctor often tells people that even when he earned $1,000,000 the first time, it disappeared quickly, and that was back in the early 60s when things were much cheaper. He often advises getting good quality financial advice. Do it before you make your millions, because you'd hate to get too busy and carried away and then wake up one day realising you should have and could have.

Handling money poorly is a paradigm; it's a habit. You can change it, but you've got to reprogram it and put things in order, so you don't need to think about it. Have it automated in a system. Set and forget.

The book *The Richest Man in Babylon* by George Clason states these seven timeless principles.

- **Start thy purse to fattening.** This principle outlines putting aside 10% of all you earn as savings, even if you're paying off debt. It's about being consistent and preparing for your future starting from today.

- **Control thy expenditures.** Don't allow your expenses to become overly inflated as you earn more. Resist the temptation to continually up the ante with your lifestyle spending.
- **Make thy gold multiply.** You don't get wealthy by working. You get wealthy by having your money earn money. Invest wisely and take advantage of time and compounding interest.
- **Guard thy treasures from loss.** While investment is essential for financial growth, it's important to remember that in almost all investments, there is the potential for loss. Balance your investments so that risk is mitigated. Essentially, don't put all your eggs in one basket and ensure you understand the risks involved with every investment.
- **Make of thy dwelling a profitable investment.** While Clason meant for this to be encouragement to own your own home, and allowing your family to thrive in it (therefore creating a feeling of abundance), these days this point is the most debatable, because many financial advisers recommend buying investments and renting, rather than buying, your own home. I'll sit this one out!
- **Insure a future income.** This point is related to preparing for unforeseen future circumstances and protecting yourself and/or your family for retirement or other financially negative situations which could come your way. In today's terms, this refers to retirement planning and income insurance.
- **Increase thy ability to earn.** You are paid what you are worth to the market (and the world). Educate and enrich your knowledge with continual learning and you will reap the rewards.

While you are fulfilling these financial goals, you will learn so much more in the process. It's not just about the money. The skills you acquire along the way will enrich you in many other ways.

Are you ready to earn more and keep growing it? I am!

Journal page

> *"Abundance is not something we acquire. It is something we tune into."* Dr Wayne Dyer

- How are you with money? What's your relationship? Does it control you, or are you in charge?

- Do you feel as though you may have a money-block or does it flow? If blocked, what do you think may be the root cause?

- What does Abundance mean to you? Is it just money? Or are there other elements for you? If so, what are they?

- What is the most you've ever earned? What's the average? Often, we can earn more money and then the following year or period, we have a correction. How about you? And how much would you love to earn?

- Often, a lack of abundance is attached to our internal self-image. How is your own self-belief, self-worth, and self-confidence?

- What other sources of revenue do you have, or would you like to have? Investments? Property? Stocks? Other businesses? MSIs (multiple sources of income)

- Millionaire traits are: Focus, Discipline & Decision-making. How do you stack up? What else do you think a millionaire does to be successful and is this a status you'd like to achieve?

Super-Charged Freedom

Abundance

Super-Charged Freedom

Self-Care

"We can't practise compassion with others, if we can't treat ourselves kindly," says Brené Brown. She goes on to say, "If walking a mile in someone else's shoes is a way to describe the concept of empathy, then self-compassion is almost like learning how to tie them in the first place. Self-compassion is the key to practising empathy for others. You need to learn how to do one before you can truly do the other."

"I'm so busy"

Modern society celebrates busyness. "I'm so busy," is one of the most heard phrases today. People are hustling, working 60-70 hours a week, pulling all-nighters, pushing themselves to burnout, all to try and "make it work".

If you live like this, like many other men on the planet, it's important to understand that this has an impact, not only on you, but on your families and those around you. If you are constantly pushing and hustling, you don't allow time to dream and create visions of something better for yourself. Besides, who wants money and "success" if you're just too damn tired to enjoy it?

Giving yourself time and space allows you time to decide if what you have been working towards is actually important. Many of the things we are working towards – cars, houses, boats – will not make us happy. People desire them because they believe the having of those things will make them happy, but it is far from true. I'm yet to meet a person who has been fulfilled by their material possessions, and in fact, those who do focus on the attainment of these things will always want the next shiny new thing immediately after. Once they buy the items, their incessant desire for new objects kicks in again, and they want just one more thing. The pursuit of material objects is insatiable.

When you get clearer on doing the work for yourself and become more focused on improving your internal self-image, you may find that your need to buy things starts to dissipate. As a recovering shopaholic myself, I have more recently found myself walking out of shops without purchases, because I've asked myself some tough questions about what was driving me to pull out my wallet in the first place.

For example, if you desire a Porsche, what do you feel the car would give you? Status, confidence, power, happiness, thrill, or excitement are pretty common desires. People believe that by having the car, they will feel these things. And to be sure, driving a flashy car can be lots of fun – but you might be surprised to learn that many people who drive these cars are just as fucked up as the rest of us. They have all the same issues and all the same worries as a guy driving last century's Hyundai. The people driving those cars who *are* happy found the key to happiness elsewhere – inside themselves – and the car was just a fun thing for them to drive around.

The lesson here is that allowing yourself time and space to just "be" is integral to going to the next level in your life. It might seem counterintuitive to get more by doing less, but I assure you it's true. I recently saw a quote from George Monbiot that said, "If wealth was the inevitable result of hard work and enterprise, every woman in Africa would be a millionaire."

So, if hard work doesn't get us there, what will?

Self-care will go a long way to getting you started. It's no coincidence that all your best ideas pop into your head in the shower, during a run, or in the pool. Our mind is zoned out or focused on something which is primarily a physical activity and not taking up valuable thinking and creative space.

This is where the magic happens.

If you spend time in nature, relaxing, taking part in hobbies and sports you love, or even just daydreaming, ideas and inspiration about how you want to live your life, and what you can do to get there, ideas will appear. These ideas happen when you least expect it, rather than when you schedule 20 minutes into your day for "brainstorming good ideas".

Feel grateful for what you have, enjoy your surroundings, appreciate your loved ones, see the beauty in small things ... and the more you feel relaxed, happy, and grateful, the more you will attract things, people, and situations into your life which inspire more relaxation, happiness, and gratitude.

What I do to relax

Mountains, beach, movies, playing with my son. There are many things I enjoy doing, but most of all I love getting outside and enjoying fresh air and exercising. It's hard to not feel grateful when you're activating endorphins.

One of my favourite things to do in summer is to pair a mountain climb with a beach swim. The contrast between the effort of walking up a mountain in the heat, followed by a swim in cold ocean water is invigorating, and I usually come away with a rush of new ideas and inspiration.

When I was running a fitness facility, I used to offer to take members on hikes and climbs once a month. After one climb up Mt Cooroora in Queensland (where I've competed in the King of the Mountain race, three years' running), we drove to Noosa and walked through the National Park, finishing up with a splash around in the Fairy Pools, which are connected to some beautiful cliffside scenery and stunning turquoise waters.

It was a great day and everything went to plan. We brought kids along too and they loved it; in fact, many of the young ones were able to climb quicker and easier than the adults. At the end of the day, when we were walking through Alexandra Bay to get to the Fairy Pools, I forgot to warn everyone that it's a nudist beach, and not the uber-cool, sexy type you might discover in Europe. It's generally frequented by overweight men in the company of other men. I think it's great that people have somewhere to go and not get arrested for their naturalist preferences, but the kids couldn't stop pointing and yelling, "I can see his willy!" and all the parents were completely floored with laughter.

These unexpected, funny moments don't happen when you are chained to your computer and focusing all your energy on chasing the next dollar.

Why is time out important?

Think of taking a break as a form of turning your computer off and on — that secret fix for when your computer is not working properly. The same goes for you.

When you start to feel fogged or blocked or overwhelmed or burnt-out, stop what you're doing and do something that helps you have a release from this pressure or stress. I'm not saying you need to quit for the day – although that can be a good idea at times – I'm suggesting you just have a breather. Go for a walk. Watch a TV show or movie that makes you happy (not a doco about serial killers.) Read a book that uplifts you. Catch up for a coffee and a quick chat with someone who inspires you. Essentially, I want you to replace those negative feelings with positive ones.

To help you really understand the importance of taking time out, some of the top producers I know, including my old bosses (Brad and Jason of Trainer HQ) would book their holidays in advance and schedule in time for breaks. This is in addition to weekend getaways. This does a few things. Firstly, it says "I matter" and it also gives you a target that you don't need to do anything else for. It gives you a sense of enjoyment knowing that this is an event to look forward to and reward yourself for all the energy and effort you're putting into the business or job.

If you want more happiness and fulfilment in your life, take more time off. Book holidays and breaks in advance. Doing this means you've always got something to look forward to, and you're ensuring that you will take time to recharge your batteries.

Some self-care ideas

It's not uncommon for people to lack ideas of how to enjoy time off. They are so used to working the grind, getting by, pushing themselves, that true relaxation time is few and far between. I've asked clients what they would do in their spare time, if they could do anything or go anywhere, and many will respond, "I don't know. I haven't thought about it, and I never have time anyway." If you can relate to this, here are a few suggestions for what you could do during some downtime.

- Yoga/Pilates/stretching.
- Exercise; walking, running, gym, HIIT, weights.
- Water sports like stand-up paddle boarding, snorkelling, jet-skiing.
- Hiking/mountain climbing.
- Coffee/drinks.
- Lunch/dinner.
- Beach/swim.
- Movies/TV shows (uplifting).
- Massage/spa treatments.
- Shopping (to a budget).
- Holiday (locally or overseas).

Journal page

> *"Talk to yourself like you would someone you love."* Brené Brown

- What excuses do you use for yourself to not have a self-care routine? List them out, then decide which ones you will not accept.
- Do you understand the importance of timeout? What does it mean to you? What things would you like to do?
- You can't pour from an empty cup. List some self-care ideas you'd like to try and choose one of these to start doing today.
- Are you booking in holidays ahead of time every year? Where would you like to go, what would you do and who would you like to do it with, and why?
- Time is your only commodity, not money, not things. If time was of the essence, what would you choose to do for yourself?

Super-Charged Freedom

Self-Care

Super-Charged Freedom

Freedom

This is what I've learned so far

A friend who worked in merchant banking in London for many years shared a story about her manager. An ambitious, driven guy, he burned the candle at both ends as an Analyst for three years, then an Associate, and later, a Vice President. He was well-known – like many of his colleagues – to indulge in certain illegal powdery substances, to give him the stamina he needed.

His goal was to be the youngest Senior Vice President in history. On the day of his promotion, he celebrated by taking his entire team out to a fancy restaurant for lunch. After a few hours of eating, drinking, and celebrating – no doubt on the expense account of a client – they returned to the office.

An hour later, his secretary walked in to find him slumped over his desk, dead at the age of 30.

He was working towards riches, status, and power, but did he have freedom?

Freedom is imperative to humans. Everyone has a different view of what freedom is. To me, it's being able to do what you want, when you want, and being able to help people by donating or helping out causes I believe in, on a regular basis.

Freedom is important to me, and with what I've been through and learnt on my way, I've developed a great grasp on it. That's why I decided to call my coaching company "Freedom Coaching".

As a twenty or thirty-something, I would often imagine my impending wealth and all the time I would have to relax and do whatever I desired; yet the behaviour and habits I was displaying were anything but those of someone who understood how to obtain this. I knew "consciously" how to imagine and daydream, but these were hopes and wishes that I managed to thwart every time. I was either not emotionally committed to them, or I made an initial decision to pursue something, and would immediately hit the infamous "terror barrier"; the invisible wall that shows itself anytime we decide to change a paradigm and replace the old program with this new idea. We start hearing all the doubts, worries, fear, and excuses.

As soon as I earned decent money or moved towards achieving my goals, I would run. That analogy we've been using as our caveman instinct – the fight or flight – is just as real in our mind as in the physical world. These days, rather than sabre-tooth tigers, we're running from obstacles, personal challenges, and perceived emotional threats. If you have set out to achieve big goals you haven't reached, then I'm sure you've done it, too.

When you try something new – like sticking to your plan and persisting despite perceived obstacles – your confidence may be drowned out by that loud, critical, inner voice, trying to talk you out of the awesome decision you've made. Don't let it. Stand your ground. Ask for help. Get someone to hold you accountable.

Freedom is so close for any person who decides it's time to take action. Freedom doesn't come from money and things. People with financial wealth can be just as miserable and trapped as somebody with a negative bank balance. Freedom actually comes from becoming the person you need to become, enjoying the ride, and opening yourself up to emotional abundance so that you can enjoy the financial freedom you create.

Creating this freedom requires patience. This doesn't mean sitting back and taking it slow. It means accepting that it will take time and practise to shed your old habits and embrace your new way of being, and the bigger and broader your goals are, the more small adjustments you will need to make. Growing into your more evolved self will take time – how much time depends on how quickly you can get yourself into the state of assuming belief of your future self as already here.

There will be tests, there will be people trying to bring you back to reality, there will be naysayers, there will be all sorts of tests, but this is YOUR life and for the purposes of these lessons, let's say that you only get one crack. I waited way too long to really understand and apply Bob's lessons. I don't plan on EVER going back to the old life. Why? Because it wasn't living; it wasn't freedom. I'm not saying my life was bad, it just wasn't truly serving me, my son, my mum, or my future girlfriend/wife.

"The cave you fear to enter holds the treasure you seek"

This is far more than just my favourite quote.

For the many years I've loved it, I didn't always understand what it really meant. For me, it represented a big, scary goal that somebody was afraid to tackle, such as starting a business or reaching for a significant promotion. My focus was always on something outside of myself, and the quote gave me confidence that if I just faced my fear of doing something new, that something magnificent would come out of it.

What I didn't realise was that the cave was never outside of me. The cave is inside. It's your own limitations or shortcomings, the part of yourself that you are afraid to examine and tackle head-on. For me, that was my dishonesty. Dishonesty primarily with myself, which resulted in not facing where I wasn't showing up in life, or where I was letting myself down. Dishonesty always towards others, when I didn't want to speak my truth out loud in case they reacted negatively. I didn't admit to myself where I was ignoring growth opportunities and instead, was hiding in bravado and bullshit. I was too scared of facing my damaged self-image. I was too scared to enter my internal cave and break through the terror barrier of change.

Today, I'm metaphorically in a different world. Diving into my internal cave has resulted in uncomfortable yet spectacular growth as a person, and the treasure I have found is valuable beyond measure. If you go headfirst into your own "cave" I can assure you there is only joy when you break through. It may not be comfortable going in at first – it wasn't for me – but it definitely gets easier, especially when your subconscious realises you're not going to quit this time; you're all in.

Are you getting ready for the adventure?

Ideas of how to free yourself

My journey is unlikely to be the one you want to emulate, so let's look at some possibilities and how you can obtain your version of freedom.

Starting with the action points from Chapter 1, let's set a goal.

What do you want? I mean, what do you truly want? Remember, you need to be excited at the prospect of achieving it and also scared by the fact it feels so big and outrageous.

Once you've made that "committed" decision, you need to make a list. I'll give you some ideas:

- What will I need to give up to be the person I need to be in order to reach my goal?

- What paradigms or poor/negative habits will I need to replace?

- Am I willing and able? (If not, maybe it's the wrong goal.)

- Do I have all the necessary knowledge to get me to my goal?

- If the last answer is no, then who can help me? Find a coach or a mentor! Even if you have a coach in your life, successful people hire different coaches and mentors for different areas of focus.

- Start creating a plan. It won't be a complete plan, because if it is, your goal is too small. Make it bigger.

- Create your goal as an affirmation and state in detail what you want, when you want to complete it by (date), and also what you're prepared to give in return. This could be the fabulous service rendered, it could be donating to charity, it could be anything that gives value to others. You can't expect to receive something without first giving – it's impossible.

- Keep a positive mental attitude by reading daily, listening to positive material, sharing with likeminded people, join a mastermind, get someone as an accountability partner.

This is not an exhaustive list, and you may want to add some of your own ideas, but those above have served me well so far and I'm sure they will for you too.

What's next?

ACTION! You have the learnings and now you know that what you want is possible. Follow the above steps; remove those paradigms that aren't serving you (in fact, they are probably controlling you, like they were me).

It may be difficult to start, and you might want to quit, multiple times. But don't just take my word for it – hundreds of others I've worked with, studied with, and spoken to, have blasted through terror barriers, stripped away unhelpful paradigms, and smashed the ceilings which previously held them in.

When you make the decision to FINALLY be successful, an immediate wall can appear before you. Why? It's the battle of your conscious and subconscious that occurs when you decide to commit to an idea. You start emotionalising, and the feelings inside can trigger fear and resistance.

The great news is, you will get used to it and you'll keep reminding yourself, "I am growing." It's the growing pains of you strengthening your mind. Just like building muscles in the gym, it follows that this process is "no pain, no gain". If at some point it's not a struggle, you're probably not growing. It won't all be uphill, but you will certainly encounter some uncomfortable moments.

Let's all build mental muscle together!

Remember, I'm only a few steps ahead of you. Reach out to me. I'd love to help you. If you've read this book and it's inspired you, maybe it's time we talk?

Email brett@brettdscott.com
Website www.superchargedfreedom.com

Journal page

> *"The great revolution in the history of man, past, present and future, is the revolution of those determined to be free."* John F Kennedy (35th President of the United States)

- What does freedom look like for you? How will you know when you've got it?

- Do you know what beliefs, habits and other characteristics you'll require to set yourself free? List them here.

- What will life look like once you've reached your "freedom"? Draw a picture. Where are you living? What do you do with your days? Do you travel? Are you doing exciting hobbies?

- Often what holds us back from living a life of Freedom is something that's inside our cave that we fear to enter. List out some possible internal triggers, past traumas, or limiting beliefs that could be that for you.

- How long have you been wanting Freedom? How important is it? Will you take action to live your very best life?

- What is your plan of attack? How are you going to get started? What do you need to ensure your success? Start the plan and then move into inspired action.

If part of your plan is to hire a coach or a mentor, perhaps it's time you reached out to me to discuss your desires and if I believe I can help, I will give you the game-plan.

Freedom

Super-Charged Freedom

AFTERWORD

I've known Brett the past few years and have been blessed to be a guest expert for him in his mastermind programs, helping his clients understand my own perspective on Freedom by sharing the very real journey I've had in discovering the true meaning for myself.

When Brett asked me to write the afterword for his new book, I immediately said yes. Not just because he asked, but for the fact that this book is meant to help people understand a recipe for success that he has implemented for himself and many hundreds of his own clients.

Freedom means different things for all of us, but for me it means balance between what others deem as our professional and personal life. I like to differentiate these a bit, I divide everything into two categories: activity I get paid for and activity I do not get paid for. What I have learned to do often is overlap these activities, such as bringing my wife with me to an international speaking engagement or bringing my son on our company trip to The Masters in Augusta, and ensure that I am never losing sight of the "non-negotiables" in my calendar. Not everyone agrees with my idea of a weighted balance in terms of priorities, but this approach allows people to better understand their personal, experiential, giving, and receiving values, and make key decisions according to those values.

Before the global financial crisis of 2008 I had amassed a personal net worth of more than $100 million dollars. Due to surrounding myself with the wrong people, ideas, and decisions, I lost touch with the values that had brought me success. It resulted in losing all of that money and I was eveon on the verge of losing my wife, as well. When I finally came to terms with what had transpired and took accountability for what had happened, I understood that my ego had been Edging Goodness Out of my life. Being forced to take stock in who I was and who I wanted to become has led me to living a values-based existence. Now, I live in a world of more than enough, where there is more than enough of everything to make everyone happy, healthy, wealthy, and worthy.

That experience has not only helped me to recoup my wealth, but discover my true calling of empowering over 1 billion people to be happy. That is my version of Super Charged Freedom.

My advice to you going forward is re-read this book, take notes in the pages provided to remember, recollect, and reengineer some of all of the ideas shared. Most importantly, create a plan of action for yourself in order to take your purpose to the next level. Create positive habits and invest in your own potential. Find coaches or mentors who sit in a position you want to be in and ask them for help or directions in getting there. Freedom comes from consistently and persistently enjoying your pursuit of your potential, so go out there and pursue it.

David Meltzer

Co-founder of Sports 1 Marketing, best-selling author, and top business coach

ABOUT THE AUTHOR

Brett D. Scott is a multi award winning, metaphysical mindset coach, bestselling author & TEDx Talk speaker who has discovered success, true success and freedom at an older age. Older than he was expecting to be, when having worked it out. Probably like many others in the world and hence why Brett began and continues to pursue this mission by delivering this book. The book he was guided to write almost 8 years prior, during his biggest breakdown moment of his life.

Since Brett started his own journey of self discovery, personal healing and decision to pay it forward and positively impact others to experience the same, he has had one main focus. Genuinely, truthfully, vulnerably help others.

Since 2019, Brett has been doing just that. Focusing on his own improvement consistently and persistently and ensuring he's sharing that with his audience and clients daily.

Brett has just upgraded his business Freedom Coaching to take on the trading name 'Super Charged Freedom', yes, the title of this book. He now has a team of people helping his clients with their breakthroughs and numerous incredible transformations. that those individuals who've experienced them would attribute part of that success to Brett's help or involvement.

Such accolades and outcomes as; Emmy & Hollywood Music in Media awards. Rookie of the Year award in business (change of careers.) Sporting MVP & Best&Fairest. Double, Triple, TenX incomes. First & upgraded homes. The list goes on...

You can reach Brett at **www.superchargedfreedom.com** or **info@brettdscott.com** directly, if you're inspired to continue your journey, after reading this book.

THE GARDEN (Poem by Wendy A. Scott)

There is this most beautiful garden. It has been nurtured and loved, well maintained, healthy and glowing. The colours of the flowers are rich and vibrant. When one enters this garden they are filled with peace and love. It is a place of calm, one where you are filled with the magic of being alive.

One day, the one who has been nurturing this wonderful garden, leaves. Slowly weeds start to come up. Over time, they take over and the garden disappears. It is now totally neglected and forgotten.

The owner has decided to go on a journey to see what is on the outside of the garden. As he gets further and further away, he begins to forget where he started. Over time he becomes so very weary from his experiences and travels, he becomes despondent and unhappy.

A memory stirs somewhere deep within him, of a beautiful place where he once lived.

One day he walks past the place he started from and as the wind blows, it parts the weeds, and he catches a glimpse of flowers growing. He walks toward the weeds, pushes his way through and sees before him a wonderful garden, amidst all the debris and begins to remember what it was like.

He now decides to get some tools and start clearing away the weeds and debris, as he does this work, he feels the peace and contentment filling up inside him, he has now realised; he is the garden and he's begun to bloom in the light.

So please all of us remember, the flower that we are, the garden that we are, for we are the light and the beauty of all that is there.

We are 'The Garden of Eden'

www.ingramcontent.com/pod-product-compliance
Lightning Source LLC
Chambersburg PA
CBHW020322010526
44107CB00054B/1943